praise for getting to amen!

"*Getting to Amen* is a splendid book full of useful advice for churches and their members to manage conflict and communicate effectively about difficult issues. Lora-Ellen McKinney constructively applies negotiation theory in concrete and practical ways that help transform conflicts into opportunities for learning, creativity, and mutual gain."

—Steve Reifenberg,
Former Latin American Program Director,
Conflict Management Group
Current Director of the Chile Regional Office,
David Rockefeller Center for Latin American Studies

"Dr. McKinney's book will be of great interest to anyone who cares about peaceable resolutions to conflict. *Getting to Amen* is not just for African Americans of conscience but for all of us who wish to become more fulfilled spiritually."

—Bruce Weinstein, The Ethics Guy
Author of *Life Principles: Feeling Good by Doing Good*

getting to amen
8 strategies for
managing conflict
in the african american church

LORA-ELLEN McKINNEY

JUDSON PRESS
PUBLISHERS SINCE 1824

VALLEY FORGE

GETTING TO AMEN
8 Strategies for Managing Conflict in the African American Church

Judson Press has made every effort to trace the ownership of all quotes. In the event of a question arising from the use of a quote, we regret any error made and will be pleased to make the necessary correction in future printings and editions of this book.

Bible quotations in this volume, as specified, are from *The Holy Bible*, King James Version (KJV); HOLY BIBLE: *New International Version* (NIV), copyright © 1973, 1978, 1984 by International Bible Study. Used by permission of Zondervan. All rights reserved; and the New Revised Standard Version of the Bible (NRSV), copyright © 1989 by the Division of Christian Education of the National Council of the Churches of Christ in the United States of America. Used by permission. All rights reserved.

Library of Congress Cataloging-in-Publication Data
McKinney, Lora-Ellen.
    Getting to amen : 8 strategies for managing conflict in the African American church / Lora-Ellen McKinney.—1st ed.
        p. cm.
ISBN 0-8170-1477-2 (alk. paper)
1. African American churches. 2. Church controversies—African American churches. 3. Conflict management—Religious aspects—Christianity. I. Title.
BR563.N4M3524 2005
254—dc22
                                                                        2005002483

Printed in the U.S.A.

13 12 11 10 09 08 07 06 05

10 9 8 7 6 5 4 3 2 1

To my maternal grandmother,

Laura Lee Stewart Jones,

who saw God through the eyes

of his children.

foreword

For more than a century, the black church has been the beacon of hope for millions of black folk bombarded by white supremacy, social injustice, and economic inequality. It has also been a haven for those in search of solutions to their spiritual and personal crises. The black church has stretched open its arms to embrace the downcast and the upwardly mobile, the single mother and her child and the nuclear family, the drug addict and the corporate executive, the lowly and the lofty. Thus, the black believer comes to church to escape social stress and cultural conflict. While parishioners are often successful in fleeing the harsh burdens of the world, they just as often confront conflict once they walk through the sanctuary doors.

We have done a far greater job beating back the demons of social oppression than we have in confronting conflicts within the black church's borders. As we have matured and prospered as a people, and as we have gained surer footing in a culture that once denied our humanity—and in some ways still does—we have experienced increasing differences in our goals, outlooks, moral ambitions, and social struggles. Even the Scripture suggests that one's experience—what one sees and hears—depends on where one stands: "Some heard thunder, and some the voice of God" (John 12:28-9, paraphrase).

Some of us believe that while racism continues to riddle our lives, we nevertheless have enormous opportunity to thrive. Some of us contend that the remarkable advances we have achieved as a people should only strengthen our resolve to make room at the table of opportunity for millions more. Some folk believe that the gospel limits the roles women can play in church; others believe that the gospel encourages women to breathe the same air of liberty as men. Some believe that the gospel speaks clearly against the theological embrace of homosexuality, while others maintain that the Good News offers love and support to gays and lesbians.

Besides these cutting-edge social problems that threaten to divide the black church in seething conflict, there are organizational and procedural problems that are equally vexing. Should the lion's share of the church's power rest in the hands of the minister or with the church's boards? And where does the congregation's will find its true voice when church leaders cite Scripture to warn against biblical examples of the people missing—even avoiding—God's guidance? And should the Bible or the business journal supply methods for raising money and procuring capital to support the church's mission?

These and a thousand more conflicts dot the internal landscape of contemporary black churches. Lora-Ellen McKinney's book, *Getting to Amen*, is a powerful examination of the underlying conflicts that produce rancor, but little resolution, in our churches. She weds the best theological principles we have produced in our ranks to the most sophisticated insights of conflict resolution. She helps us to address how black churches can identify, cope with, and even transform problems that, when left to fester, can stall or stalemate black church progress.

One of the hallmark beauties of her book is the insistence that we don't have to surrender our principled stands on critical issues to work beyond our differences—or even through them—to embrace one another as brothers and sisters in Christ. This book is much more than a theoretical interpretation of the principles that regulate the negotiation of potentially fatal divisions in ecclesiastical life. It is also, and perhaps most important, a practical handbook to resolve conflicts that, when addressed in a healthy fashion, can lead to a deepening of our theological insight while strengthening our mission to change the world through love.

—Michael Eric Dyson
Avalon Foundation Professor in the Humanities
and Professor of African-American
and Religious Studies,
University of Pennsylvania

introduction

I've been in the storm so long
I've been in the storm so long
Oh Lord, give me more time to pray,
I've been in the storm so long.[1]

CHURCHES HAVE BECOME BATTLEFIELDS. FROM THE MORE COM-
mon territorial clashes that have always taken place in choir
rooms or among the deacons to the statements that many ministers make from pulpits to galvanize congregations or communities for
or against highly political and controversial issues, churches increasingly
find themselves in conflict. Rather than working together peaceably to
advance the recommendations and expectations of the Great Commission, preachers, church leaders, and parishioners often work to get their
individual needs met or to advance their own agendas. The result is conflict. If there is no loving way to resolve the issues about which we differ,
conflict in Christ's house can only make for an unholy mess.

African American churches have always provided parishioners and
community members with a special place in which they could feel safe
and affirmed, even when the outside world denigrated them and
denied them opportunity. For preachers, the pulpit has also historically been—and continues to be—a coveted job, representing both an
opportunity to assist the community and a source of individual and
corporate power in the African American subculture. When African
Americans, who are so denied in the world, have taken their burdens
to the Lord and left them there, the church doors have always swung
open on wonderfully welcome hinges.

*Getting to Amen: 8 Strategies for Managing Conflict in the African
American Church* was born out of concerns about how conflict has

affected the African American church. The negative components of conflict are increasingly present in our churches and, in many cases, neither preachers nor parishioners have the requisite skills necessary to move smoothly from conflict and chaos to Christ.

I began to get some strong hints of the problems resulting from unmanaged conflict while conducting research for my book *View from the Pew: What Preachers Can Learn from Parishioners* and in the reports I typically receive during workshops I conduct around my book *Christian Education in the African American Church: A Guide for Teaching Truth*. Signs of unhealthy conflict are also evident from what I observe and hear as I sit in congregations around the country. And, in addition to polarizing society, the 2004 election year created conflict in churches around a number of faith, social, and political issues.

Struggles in our personal lives lead to conflict. Divorce ends more than half of American marriages. Suicide, self-injury, depression, and substance abuse are increasing in all demographic groups in our country as wounded souls in internal conflict seek to end it, cut it out, hide it in dark places, or self-medicate against it. People who are angry and conflicted in their personal lives bring their hurts to the church. This is, of course, as it should be, for Christ is the salve that we all seek.

What should never happen, though, is for us to allow personal hurts to run amok in the life of the church. Nor should we allow the church to become a haven for new conflicts. Unfortunately, in African American churches, many of us struggle to claim our committee work and tasks as our own territory,[2] often, perhaps subconsciously, seeking the power that has been denied us outside the church's walls.

addressing conflict

Getting to Amen presents ways to work through the conflict that is inevitable when God's people bring their problems together. Chapter 5 expounds upon eight strategies for managing conflict in the African American church, strategies I refer to throughout as the "8 P's": prayer, preaching, parishioner awareness, perspective(s) on problems, practical solutions, programs and premises, pastoral management, and promises. While the 8 P's model can work for all types of conflict—and, as we will see, conflict is natural and not in and of itself a bad thing—*Getting to Amen* focuses on topics, including women in church leadership and church migration, that churches are finding particularly challenging to manage without conflict.

The book is divided into three sections. Section One: "Managing Conflict—A Primer" provides a brief historical overview of conflict resolution theories. Section Two, "Applying the Strategies to Issues," presents specific topics that create conflict, over which this book's problem-solving model is overlaid with explicit recommendations. The goal is not to prove anyone right or wrong, but to provide counsel for working our way through the various conflict-creating issues. Section Three, "Going Forward from Here," is at once a look backward and forward. This section briefly recaps why getting to Amen is necessary and then presents a concept that takes readers beyond what the individual church can do to address conflict.

getting to amen as a tool for change

The title of this book, *Getting to Amen* is a reference to the famous book by Roger Fisher, William Ury, and Bruce Patton entitled *Getting to Yes: Negotiating Agreement without Giving In.* A product of the Harvard Negotiation Project, the *Getting to Yes* project is used as a "universally applicable method for negotiating personal and professional disputes without getting taken—and without getting angry." It has been successfully used as a strategic tool for solving business and political challenges in the United States and around the world. It addresses the meaning and limits of principled negotiations, doling out practical rather than moral advice to its readers. The excellent ideas presented in *Getting to Yes* include adherence to the following rubric:

The Problem: Don't bargain over positions.[3]

The Method: Separate the people from the problem.[4] Focus on interests, not positions.[5] Invent options, not mutual gain.[6] Insist on using objective criteria.[7]

The *Getting to Yes* team also recognizes that there are times when one group actually holds more power than the other team. In these cases, it recommends that groups develop their Best Alternative to a Negotiated Agreement (BATNA). But even such a well-respected model does not necessarily take into account some of the specific needs of religious communities, or of the very particular needs of the black church. *Getting to Amen* addresses these needs, providing readers with methods for negotiating conflict in the African American church.

This book is intended for a broad readership, including seminarians, established clergy, and lay readers committed to improving the church because they, as do I, love the Lord and are committed to helping the church of God grow into an institution that is all that it should be. It addresses strategies by which pastors, church leaders, and congregations can solve problems. The book answers these questions: When the unity of the local church body is at risk of being compromised by internal conflict, how should we respond? How should our churches address conflict-raising social issues? What are the most effective methods for negotiating conflict in the church? What does our future hold if we do not address these issues now?

Getting to Amen offers questions, presented under the title "Taking Off the Shackles," which are designed to help local congregations assess their strengths and weaknesses relative to various issues highlighted throughout the book. The questions are also designed to help individuals and congregations move forward, not just in the short-term, but also in the planning of long-term strategies to maintain and strengthen God's church. These questions can be used to stimulate discussion in Christian education classes or as fodder for personal prayer. Because our hearts and our minds can be shackled, and it is essential that our futures not be, these questions are designed to be provocative and thought provoking, as well as prayerful.

embracing conversation

Based on a set of principles for managing conflict and creating change, this book assumes that those who read it are committed to making God's house a place where God's people can worship, work, and live together in peace. On some specific topics, readers will have divergent viewpoints. However, if those who disagree share the goal of an open discussion that allows each side to be heard, no more can be asked.

It is my fervent prayer that this book will help churches communicate effectively about difficult issues in ways that are beneficial to members, the local church, and the church of God; in ways that facilitate effective problem-solving and conflict management, leading to long-term solutions; in ways that spark the creation of innovative church policies and programs that address those solutions; and in ways that lead to a community dedicated to God, one that eagerly embraces the challenge of Christ-focused change.

The African American church has historically been and continues to be our strongest institution. But it is also an institution that, as a result of finances poorly managed, egos run amok, congregational splits, and dogmatic and denominational shifts, has significantly weakened over the last decade. *Getting to Amen* aspires to provide a set of practical tools to help our churches move beyond misunderstandings to Hallelujah moments, from chaos and conflict to Christ, so that together as a community of disciples we can get to harmonious and peaceable AMENs!

managing
conflict—a primer

1

what the tribe needs to know

Now I beseech you, brethren, by the name of our Lord
Jesus Christ, that ye all speak the same thing, and that there
be no divisions among you; but that ye be perfectly joined
together in the same mind and in the same judgment.
—1 Corinthians 1:10, KJV

DESPITE EVIDENCE THAT OUR CHURCHES ARE ATTRACTING NEW
members in record numbers,[1] issues such as female leadership
in the church, homosexuality, loss of denominational identity, church splits within denominations, nontraditional interpretations of Scripture, and cross-faith ecumenical activities have polarized
mainline Protestant denominations and have most certainly caused
rends within the African American church. Other issues of importance
include the role of the church in an increasingly multicultural world
and the church's response to sociological realities, including homeless-
ness, domestic violence, child physical and sexual abuse, community
health, sexually transmitted diseases such as HIV/AIDS, and domestic
and international terrorism.

Conflict is part of human nature, having existed since Adam and
Eve had their argument about whether or not God gave them permission to eat that appealing piece of fruit in the Garden of Eden.
Throughout history, human conflicts have arisen most often from
needs related to territoriality. The survival of the human species, in the
earliest days of human kind, depended on the ability to establish and
protect territory.[2] The specifics have changed, but these dynamics
remain relevant in our modern era and lead to anger and aggression,

ranging from interpersonal relationship problems to tribal conflicts to organized wars[3] to genocide.

conflict defined

Conflicts are complex creatures, taking place among persons and groups in historical contexts and times, and are related to specific sets of issues. To understand the nature of conflicts, we must first define "conflict," specify its source, and evaluate its functional and dysfunctional consequences. According to Goodwin Watson and David Johnson, a conflict exists whenever incompatible activities occur; an action which is incompatible with another action prevents, obstructs, interferes with, injures, or in some way makes that action less likely or less effective. The incompatible actions may originate in one person (intrapersonal), one group (intragroup), two or more persons (interpersonal), or two or more groups (intergroup). A conflict may arise from several sources, some of which are (1) differences in information, belief, values, interests, and desires; (2) a scarcity of some resource such as power, money, time, space, and position; and (3) rivalries in which one person or group competes with another.[4]

According to this definition, while the African American church is as likely as any other church to have conflicts arising from the incompatible actions and activities of persons or groups, we can at least take hope that there are relatively few differences in the area of belief. While some churches may have conflicts over dogma, African American churches are more likely to experience conflicts relative to issues of power, position, and money—issues that fall into the second and third categories of the above definition.

It is important (and not accidental) that this is so. Given the history of African Americans in this country, the African American church has historically been the one place where status, in the form of power and position (and to a certain degree, money), has been available to African Americans. Black men have always found the church to be a place that afforded them respect and positions of honor, even when the society outside of the church disrespected them. Women, called Sister and Mother, are held in a special measure of respect as well.[5]

principal theories of conflict

Though it is impossible to supply all of the background research that has informed the thinking in this realm, this section provides a brief overview of the principal theories, traditional and nontraditional, regarding why conflict occurs and how it is best managed.

Before beginning the review of principal theories on conflict, however, it is important to make three statements:

1. *The opposite of conflict is attraction.* If people and/or groups get along well, there is no problem! When we like one another and see what is good in one another, then conflict does not happen (and herein may lie a strategy for conflict management).[6] We tend to like those whose beliefs and interests are similar to our own, who share our competencies and skills, who have qualities we consider admirable, and who like us in return.[7]

2. *We can like one another and be in conflict at the same time.* Successful married couples and good friendships must navigate the shifting shoals of emotion over time. Think about how every parent feels about his or her beloved children when they get into trouble! People get angry, work through their problems and, hopefully, get over them. But while we are in the conflict, we like and even love the person who presents the problem for us.

3. *Conflict is not necessarily negative.* Conflict is not always an all-out war. It is sometimes how people learn from one another. Ultimately, it can, if properly managed, lead to growth.

In her book *Church Conflict: From Contention to Collaboration*, Norma Cook Everist provides the following characteristics of destructive conflict and productive conflict.[8] Characteristics of destructive conflict include: voices are silenced and people regularly avoid each other; the atmosphere is one of sadness, apathy, or merely strained civility; people harbor resentments, remembering when they were slighted; rumors have been replaced by acrimonious rancor; members are dissatisfied with outcomes, feeling only that they have lost; and faith is squashed and people leave not only the congregation, but never return to any church. Characteristics of productive conflict include: people feel their voices, although diverse, are heard; people's fears are addressed and are allayed; people are growing in courage and confidence and have a positive sense of self; people are seeking to become more informed about various options and understand one another better; people are willing to share power; the atmosphere is stimulating and people begin to care more about issues and others; people are demonstrating faith in a God active in human encounter.

Sigmund Freud, the father of psychoanalysis, believed individual personalities to be like icebergs, with our most important personality processes occurring below the level of conscious awareness in the same way that an iceberg exists mainly below the surface of the water. Conflicts were thought to emerge in clashes between and among three portions of the personality (the id, ego, and superego)[9] and when ideas, urges, and behaviors that had been below the personality's surface came into consciousness. Though most of Freud's work and theory focused on the individual and among groups of individuals, Freud believed that conflicts, from interpersonal to international,[10] occur when "big heads" come into conflict with each other.

Social psychologist Elliott Aronson notes that in our social interactions, human beings are fascinatingly conservative; we attempt to maintain our individual and group beliefs. It is no surprise, then, that when people come together in situations where we attempt to maintain separate sets of perceptions, the potential for conflict is created.

negotiation strategies

The Harvard Negotiation Project has a number of important books, most of them based on their essential initial concept of "Getting to Yes." "Getting to Yes" begins with the understanding that people and groups must build relationships as they negotiate. It is assumed that everyone brings a valuable skill to the negotiation and, with hard work and effort, can find a way to agree without feeling as if they are giving in. It is the fear of giving in or of losing face (as well as losing the value of the item or issue that they are negotiating) that so often makes people leave the room before negotiating a successful deal. It also requires that one or both sides find ways to escalate or even create a conflict. The concept of BATNA (Best Alternative to a Negotiated Agreement) is the tool that one always has as a back-up, just in case the other team is stubborn, but the face-saving goal is the same in that each team can achieve a point on their goal list and feel as if their negotiation has been successful.

The Eastern Mennonite religious community has created mediation and conflict resolution strategies that have been used worldwide. Peaceable living is an essential component of the tenets of the Eastern Mennonite faith; conflict resolution strategies became a logical outgrowth of the work of their faith communities. Noting success in negotiating conflicts with the IRA and between the South African government and the ANC, John Paul Lederach, who developed this method and serves as the director of the International Conciliation Committee, stated that "transformative peacemaking is based on understanding fair, respectful, and inclusive process as a way of life and envisions outcome as a commitment to increasing justice, seeking truth, and healing relationships."[11] Were we all, as people of faith, to adopt within our churches such codes of peace toward one another, our world would truly be transformed.

Another well-respected conflict management method is proposed by ethicist Bruce Weinstein, syndicated newspaper columnist ("Ask the Ethics Guy"), CNN contributor, and author of *What Should I Do? 4 Simple Steps to Making Better Decisions in Everyday Life*. Dr. Weinstein proposes four steps for working through any decision-making process in which an ethical decision is required: gather the relevant facts; identify the values at stake; consider the options; and consider the best option, given the facts and values that play a role.[12] Dr. Weinstein makes the important point that any decision-making process has multiple implications, among which are costs and benefits based on the following considerations: the rights and welfare of other people; our own conduct; ethics and morals; legal complications; economic considerations; psychological issues; and relationship challenges.

When led by emotions—anger, happiness, perceived purpose—we tend to act impetuously. Before we realize it, we are often involved in emotional, legal, moral, and spiritual entanglements that, had we used the logical thought processes with which God has graced us, we would have avoided many of the problems that plague us in our personal lives and in our relationships with family, friends, workmates, and fellow congregants.

can't we all just get along?

In a famous classic experiment on intergroup conflict conducted in 1966, Dr. Muzafer Sherif tested several methods for reducing preexisting tensions between rival groups. He concluded that the groups were most likely to resolve their conflicts if they had: common goals, the accomplishment of which did not call for competition across group lines; cooperative interdependence, which, simply stated, means that to accomplish their common goals, people or groups have to cooperate with each other; equal status in the situation; the sanctions of custom, law, or authority favoring the reduction of conflict; and no misinterpretations of the opponents as confirming negative stereotypes.[13]

Based on Sherif's findings, church conflicts present unique challenges for effective problem solving. The following is an application of the previously listed goals with considerations for African American church goals and needs taken into account.

Common goals. While church groups all believe in Christ, their paths to Christ can seem different. It is most important that these groups not compete with one another. In African American churches, many of which have scarce financial resources[14] and limited power, the degree to which people are willing to put competition aside may depend on personalities, the capacity to put long-term goals over short-term gain, and natural problem-solving abilities. When people are competing for resources and power in their jobs, they would like the assurance of feeling respected and powerful in God's house.[15] Because the limited resources found in many of our churches can put considerable strain on the already stressed saints who work on various church committees and in different assigned, appointed, elected, and volunteer roles, the path to determining common goals is more often less straightforward than is desirable.

Cooperative interdependence. Similar to common goals, cooperative interdependence requires that all sides agree to behave honorably. In the case of those working on behalf of the church of God, this must be done for Christ's sake and in Christ's name. In the secular world of potentially ugly negotiations, there is no such mandate. Unfortunately, many conflicts that occur in churches indicate that church members, groups, and pastors often behave instinctually rather than spiritually.

Equal status in the situation. In our churches, most of those who sit in the pew share equal status and fight for positions of power. The senior pastor holds the highest status in the church, followed by the ministerial staff, then lay leaders such as deacons, elders, and those in charge of church departments such as the Department of Christian Education or other positions appointed by the pastor or voted on by church leaders or members.[16] Those forms of artificial status aside,[17] everyone is equal in the eyes of God. Many of us forget this beautiful fact when we walk into church.

Sanctions of custom, law, or authority favoring the reduction of conflict. When sanctions occur, there is a negative impact on churches. There will be some churches in which conflicts occur because of legal sanctions or the possibility that they will be upheld at a future date. In severe cases, intergroup conflicts in our churches lead to congregational splits. More positively, the law can work to assist in the outcome of reduced conflict as well, by creating an environment in which groups that have been at odds can work together. Typically the groups will have already worked out the functional aspects of their relationships;

these sanctions of law or authority are noted in the specific details of the documents drawn up in the aftermath of the conflict.

No misinterpretations of the opponents as confirming negative stereotypes. One of our worst behaviors as African Americans is that we have taken on behaviors that are roles in which the oppressor once placed us, and which we have since too often embraced for ourselves. This is why, in Chicago's Trinity United Church of Christ, the Rev. Dr. Jeremiah A. Wright Jr. designed a policy that the church would disallow the use of language that reinforces negative stereotypes for African Americans.[18]

getting to amen

The process of getting to Amen involves the use of effective problem solving, conflict management, negotiation, relationship building, and communication strategies that are specifically useful in the context of the African American church and culture. While conflict management tactics all share certain factors that make them successful, it is incumbent upon those who use them in Christ's name to engage the strategies in a manner that sets a much higher standard than might be used in our secular society. Additionally, it is important that the "end" of conflict management strategies have identifiable outcomes in which the goal is to strategically strengthen the local and global church in clear and significant ways.

How often have we gone to meetings to solve problems, worked through challenging issues, and wondered, "What happens now?" Most often, we have been frustrated by the experience, feeling that we have solved our conflicts or issues only in the short term. Implementing policies and programs is an essential follow-up to any successful conflict management strategy. Once problems have been solved and relationships mended, the issues that created the problems may remain. It is important that there be some way to put in place a mechanism to address the underlying problem signaled by the conflict.

understanding and reclaiming the tribe

In the book *Tribes: How Race, Religion and Identity Determine Success in the New Global Economy*, Joel Kotkin provides painstaking research that outlines the manner in which four cultural tribes—the English, the Japanese, the Chinese, and the Indians—will successfully create international dominance in the twenty-first century. Africans across the diaspora were not part of this successful network of global tribes, nor were we mentioned in the chapter on "future tribes" poised for strategic economic success. There were, for Kotkin, a set of factors that identified such success: (1) ethnic identity, (2) moral and religious values, (3) tribal trust, and (4) strong, functional families. Neither diasporic Africans nor African Americans met Kotkin's necessary criteria. We may take Kotkin's global economic assessments and predictions as a challenge to examine and enhance the constructive elements of the African American community.

Though acknowledged by the U.S.'s white majority as having made contributions in particular arenas—typically entertainment fields such as music and sports, or more rarely, politics—and for specific notable persons as varied as Martin Luther King Jr., Jesse Jackson, Paul Robeson, Condaleeza Rice, and Colin Powell—African Americans are infrequently described as contributors to the American landscape.[19] Within our culture we are more often viewed as persons who suffer disproportionately from or are responsible for a vast array of social ills that stem from poverty, among which are criminal activity, incarceration, substandard education, fractured families, and un- and underemployment. Also, while some scientists will, albeit grudgingly, give African peoples credit for being the earth's first human inhabitants,[20] as well as for having made significant historical contributions to ancient scientific fields (typically astronomy and mathematics), it is more usual that today's continental Africans are regarded as the operators of corrupt nations, the purveyors of confusing interethnic wars, and the decimators of the continent through the spread of HIV/AIDS to women and children.[21]

Honest self-assessment reveals that we cannot be credited as having entirely cohesive national or international black communities built on principles that reflect the strengths of our African heritage and that are designed to assure domestic and global sustainability. There are, obviously, some understandable historical reasons for a number of our problems. Our tribe was purposefully destabilized. The rape and pillaging of African peoples and resources (precious metals, ores, gems, and oils) have created generations-long struggles on our continents, in our communities, and, importantly and painfully, in ourselves. Events on the African continent, the more recent history of African American and Caribbean enslavement, and the consequent purposeful division of African families and language groups as an economic strategy of the British and other European tribes, contribute significantly to the present-day struggles of African peoples throughout the diaspora, and, specifically, within the United States.

Unlike the Jewish tribe, another historically oppressed group, whose singular faith, small population, and officially sanctioned shunning from particular professions forced them to expand a set of commercial trades into a variety of transportable occupations,[22] Africans have always been large in number and have come from significantly larger and more diverse geographical regions. Today, as was the case before slavery, we speak different languages, are ethnically diverse, and are of many faith traditions. Nonetheless, we share many important, consistent, and unifying beliefs—in a universal and omnipotent God, in the strength of the extended family, in the power and release present in the outward demonstration of emotions, and in the importance of personal self-expression through vehicles such as the arts.

Though, as a component of our wonderfully emotive cultural make-up, African Americans can sometimes be linguistically combative in our interpersonal relationships,[23] we are also very forgiving. Despite these significant strengths, our behaviors do not always match our values. For example, we tend to believe in the importance of family[24] but often practice behaviors, such as pregnancy outside of marriage (the new culture of "baby mamas and daddies") that mitigate against the family's cohesiveness and strength. We have, additionally, though many do not like it to be stated aloud, fallen prey to the culture of victimization,[25] hindering our capacity to use our many strengths to collectively build a future, one that overcomes our past and present challenges and positively positions us for opportunities that lend themselves to maximum community benefit.

Getting to Amen is a challenge to African American churches to honestly examine ourselves and see what actions are necessary to become all that God intends us to be. We are led straight to the doors of the church. The African American church is widely and correctly viewed as the single strongest institution in our community. A recent multiyear study conducted by the Barna Group looked at the impact of the black church on the lives of black people. It concluded: "Upon dissecting the role of faith in the lives of black Americans, we discovered that their faith in Christ has empowered millions of blacks to overcome challenges that might otherwise have been debilitating. The local church has been a major source of strength and directive leadership for the black community."[26] Though not without its own set of problems, many of which will be addressed in this book, the church is an excellent place to begin strategically rethinking ways to strengthen ourselves; change real perceptions and misperceptions; and build the local, national, and international linkages required to reclaim, in God's name and for God's sake, the purpose, vision, and potential of our tribe.

2
african american christian ethics

For I will proclaim the name of the Lord;
ascribe greatness to our God!
The Rock, his work is perfect,
and all his ways are just.
A faithful God, without deceit,
just and upright is he.
—Deuteronomy 32:3-4, NRSV

CONFLICT IN THE AFRICAN AMERICAN CHURCH OCCURS IN A VARI-
ety of ways and at many different levels. At the local church
level, unmanaged conflict produces ineffective ministry and
hurt feelings. At the national level, conflict has led to denominational splits.

In 1880, three African American conventions—the Baptist Foreign
Mission Convention, the American Baptist Convention, and the
National Baptist Educational Convention—merged to become the
National Baptist Convention. (Conventions are very important for
Baptists, as each church is an autonomous structure.) Since the establishment of the National Baptist Convention (NBC), there have been
splits over policy and political issues. Concerns over whether the NBC
publishing board should be owned by any Baptist convention or
should be free to affiliate with groups outside of the NBC led to a split
in 1915 into the NBC-USA, Inc., and the NBC of America, Unincor-
porated.[1] Arguably, the most well-known conflict within the body of
African American Baptists resulted from a dispute on the political
nature of the ministry and message of Martin Luther King Jr. during

the early days of the Civil Rights Movement. The Progressive National Baptist Convention grew from a 1961 split with NBC on this issue.

The church, as well as the African American community at large, has also experienced conflict on various social issues related to our minority status and striving for advancement in the society. This conflict was reflected by the furor caused when comedian, educator, and philanthropist Bill Cosby spoke out in the spring of 2004 about the personal responsibility the black community must take for its choices, rather than using "victimhood" excuses.

"Let me tell you something," he said. "Your dirty laundry gets out of school at 2:30 every day. It's cursing and calling each other the N-word as they're walking down the street. They think they're hip. They can't read. They can't write. They're laughing and they're giggling and they're going nowhere."[2]

This is but one of the statements Dr. Cosby made about the "ungrammatical locution and dysfunctional behavior"[3] of young African Americans. His statements received headlines in all major newspapers and were discussed by commentators of network and cable news stations. In churches, barbershops, and beauty salons, there were two primary versions of an intense conversation: (1) "How dare he!" and (2) "It's about time!"

The "How dare he!" conversation went something like this: Mr. Cosby is an incredibly wealthy man. As a multimillionaire celebrity, he is extraordinarily out of touch with those about whom he is speaking, most of whom can be assumed to live lives quite different from his. People are stuck in lower economic strata because, in spite of years of social programs for which so many of us fought in the streets, courts, and through our personal efforts on behalf of our families, the system is stacked against African Americans. According to Human Rights Watch, in the state of Washington, for example, where 3.2 percent of the citizens are African American, we are 18 percent of those incarcerated.[4] If education, job availability, and other systems that are required for our long-term survival and empowerment continue to be deficient, it is impossible for large portions of our community to advance. It is fine, of course, for us to have these discussions among ourselves. We don't like the way these kids Mr. Cosby was mentioning walk, talk, dress, and behave either, but it's not entirely their fault *and* he made these statements in places where white media were present and could easily report them. This is *our* dirty laundry, and it should be kept private.

The "It's about time!" argument acknowledges the factors described above, noting the dichotomy between Mr. Cosby's status as an exceptionally wealthy man and the challenge of dealing with increasing numbers of poor, undersocialized, urban youth. We know that the struggle for equal rights is not over, and we have no problem continuing the fight. But neither can we keep pointing the finger at the white man. The white man can bring drugs into our neighborhood—he is, at least, at the top of the drug totem pole—but if we are the local drug lords and drug runners, then we are the problem. If we sell drugs to our children, even if we need money because there are not other easily available jobs, that is a conscious choice. If we confuse educational excellence with being white, then we have made a decision not to be hired in decent jobs. While slavery, then, has created a long-term chokehold on how we have been able to make progress, we have to break away from its twenty-first-century manifestations by saying that we refuse to be choked anymore. As for white people hearing the conversation, if we are taking responsibility for ourselves, so what? Mr. Cosby told the *Milwaukee Journal Sentinel* journalist Eugene Kane that, at sixty-seven years of age, he was simply too old to care what white people think about the airing of black people's dirty laundry.[5]

core values

Differences that have divided individuals and denominations notwithstanding, African American Christians possess a set of core values. Efforts to address conflict in healthy ways must include not only rediscovering but also emphasizing these core values that are made manifest in our lives and faith.

Upon their 1619 arrival in America as slaves, most Africans were not Christian. As early as the second century, however, some Africans might have come into contact with Christianity when the Christian mission spread to Northern Africa and farther south in Africa to Nubia (see Acts 8:27).[6] European slave traders, predominantly Christian, had missionaries among them who began evangelical work on their pagan African trade as soon as they arrived on the boats. As a result of some of these exposures, though our forefathers arrived on American shores with decidedly African cultural values and mores, by the time of their arrival here some of those values may have blended with a Christian religious perspective.

Even for those who had not had direct exposure to Christianity, well-documented research indicates significant similarities in the doctrinal values of traditional African religion and Christian beliefs. Among these similarities is the view of God as omnipotent, omniscient, omnipresent, and just. "African societies had highly sophisticated cosmologies and theologies well before contact with the Europeans who would seek to destabilize these societies and enslave their members, and then go on to justify such enslavement on theological and religious grounds."[7] The core beliefs inculcated into African religious practices served multiple purposes. As theological premises, they provided the structure for worship and praise; were the focus of individual relationships with God; and served, within both forms of relationship, as sources of protection that reminded Africans, once they were enslaved, about the very nature of the God who had been with them through the Middle Passage. "No slave master taught us that God is just. We knew that very well before we came here, and there are hundreds of [African] proverbs to document this. The only new things to slaves were Jesus and Hell. The Bible had a new way of saying the rest of our basic worldview."[8]

Through this worldview, our ethical African American roots were firmly established. Ethics is defined as a code of morality or a system of moral principles governing the appropriate conduct for an individual or group.[9] The development of our worldview, from its deep historical roots in Africa through the rich manifestations of our current faith as African American Christians, relies on an implicit belief in the Holy Spirit as an ethical guide. This internalized spiritual guide helps us address conflicts as they arise in daily life, as they occur in our family and personal relationships, and as we confront those that occur on a cultural level. Together, our ethical grounding helps us confront these multiple areas of conflict, molding us in the process into a people of faith, prayer, and conscious purpose based on faith-based core beliefs.

Henry H. Mitchell and Nicholas Cooper Lewter explain that core beliefs are

> the bedrock attitudes that govern all deliberate behavior and relationships and also spontaneous responses to crises....They have been acquired through life experiences, worship, and cultural exposure, and they can be altered likewise. Core beliefs are not mere propositions to which assent is given. They are the ways in which one trusts or fails to trust. They are embraced intuitively or emotionally, with or without the ability to express them rationally.[10]

Among the core beliefs of African American Christians is that the Bible is the sourcebook of our faith. Even as we affirm this, however, we must acknowledge that the Bible itself is an area of potential conflict. Those who consider themselves conservative or fundamentalist Christians are more inclined to believe the Bible to be the literal Word of God than are more theologically liberal Christians who have an equally devout view. This distinction, admittedly very general, affects the way we interpret the Bible and what it has to say to the moral and social issues of our time. One example was the political debate over same-sex marriage and civil unions that became an agenda item during the 2004 presidential election season. Ultimately believers understand this issue differently as a result of differing views of Scripture and how it should be interpreted.

Conflict is not caused by the evaporation of our core beliefs—those beliefs do not leave us when we have crises in our lives. Rather, conflict is more likely to reflect the inconsistent implementation of our core beliefs. We forget, for example, that God is the air that we breathe, and, as a result, we are likely to create environmental abuses. We forget that our children are gifts from God, and so sometimes we subject them, through our fighting, to the most vile language and behavior, not understanding that the selfish adult need to vent, so soon over and forgotten, has scared them and scarred them, teaching them anger, aggression toward others, abusive patterns between the genders, and fear of their parents. We forget that, because God made us, we are worthy, and so we allow others to strip us of our power and our beauty.

Our core Christian beliefs, which follow, are a synopsis of the primary beliefs and values that ground our Christian walk and that, when we slip and fall, are the very same tools that we have at our disposal to pick ourselves up, with the Lord's assistance. Presented from an Afri-Christian perspective, these core beliefs stand as values that, when applied to our lives, allow us to love ourselves and one another as God loves us (see 1 John 4:19-21). Again, any understanding of how to manage conflict effectively and well requires a reminder of the underpinnings of our ethical grounding.

PEOPLE OF THE BOOK

> For the word of the LORD is upright,
> and all his work is done in faithfulness. (Psalm 33:4, NRSV)

As noted above, God speaks to us and teaches, shapes, molds, and demonstrates his love for us through the Bible. Religions of the book are those in which faith and practice have been written down as sacred texts.[11] The Bible, our sourcebook, is the text in which God's love for humanity is explained and in which a historical narration of God's acts and actors are presented, leading us from the history of the people of Israel in the Old Testament to preparation for the birth, death, sacrifice, and resurrection of Jesus Christ in the New Testament.[12] The Bible also tells instructive tales of human responses to God's requests. The range of those responses, whether rebellious, rejecting, adoring, or obedient, indicates the maturing relationship of God's people to their Maker.

Because the blood of Ham runs through us, we must be committed to relearning biblical history within its historical context and as it applies to our lives. Not only is the Bible our guidebook for how to manage our lives and our conflicts, but if we use it well, it also provides us with myriad examples, not just from the lives of the people of Israel, but also from the lives of our biblical ancestors, who came from Egypt and Cush (Ethiopia). Because maps are political tools, we have not been taught that Egypt is part of the African continent, and, until recently, even biblical maps did not routinely include Cush as a geographical area from which the descendants of Ham dispersed.[13] Most important, however, having internalized negative stereotypes about ourselves, while we identify strongly with Old Testament slaves, we have only recently begun to learn about the role of Africans in the Bible.

Core Value: The Bible is not external to us, but is *in* us.

THE CHRIST OF SUFFERING
> They hung him high
> They stretched him wide.
> He bowed his head
> And then he died.
> That's love.[14]

Christ died for our sins. As a people who have suffered much, African Americans who have empathized with the struggle of the Israelites in their bondage have also understood the travails of Christ's life and considerable suffering. The theological constructs of all Christian people include a Jesus who resembles them. This has, however, been problematic for people of African descent. After all, for the majority culture (in power)[15] a despised people must not determine that the Savior of the world has actually made them in his image, regardless of the Bible's teachings. When, for example, the *National Catholic Reporter* conducted a contest for a portrait of Jesus for the national millennium celebration and the winner, "Jesus of the People," chosen from 1,500 entries from 1,000 artists in nineteen countries and six continents, was black, the world gasped in horror at a black Christ, and the image did not become the new national representation as was planned.[16] Rejection was familiar to Christ in his time and is also a common component of the African American experience.

Remembering *why* Christ died is more important than remembering *that* he died for us. In spite of our familiarity with the history of suffering, many of us have entered the twenty-first century with a modicum of comfort. These comforts have been earned for us by our ancestors, yet we are often unappreciative of the numerous sacrifices made on our behalf. A National Public Radio story mentioned that, shortly before he died, Supreme Court Justice Thurgood Marshall lamented to his clerk, Randall Kennedy, that he feared that many had forgotten his contribution to the original civil rights struggle.[17] It is true that many don't understand the complexity of Marshall's work for civil rights (he coined the term). Some don't even know who he is. If we find it so easy to forget these sacrifices, it is even easier to forget, not *that*, but *why* Christ died for us. If it is easy for young people to forget, as they daily do, the reasons their parents work to assure that they are well-cared for, then it is easy to forget not *that*, but *why* Christ died for us.

Core Value: Christ sacrificed his life for us; daily we can make sacrifices for him.

CHRIST THE LIBERATOR
> Ride on, King Jesus
> No man can a-hinder me.
> Ride on, King Jesus, ride on.
> No man can a-hinder me,
> no man can a-hinder me.[18]

In dying for the salvation of our sins, Christ the Liberator liberated our souls. For African Americans, liberation has been and continues to be an ongoing cultural and spiritual theme. Our slave heritage reminds us of the importance of freedom in many important ways.

The narratives of slaves record in the language of our ancestors fervent wishes for liberty from cruel masters, coupled with the knowledge that Christ was the source of that freedom whether or not a temporal source of escape was available to them.

Spirituals, our slave songs, remain the best oral tradition of our firm and constant belief that the God of Israel, having already been proven as the God who could bring a people out of slavery, was (and is now) exemplified in the Son, Jesus, who having died for the sins of the world, took on a liberating mantle, bringing them and subsequent generations through both joyful and difficult times.

For our slave foreparents, liberation was an actual and an internalized spiritual balm. For those slaves unable to escape slavery through northern routes to freedom—those who were aware that they would likely lose their children to the master, be viciously whipped, raped, or otherwise brutalized at his hand—freedom of the heart and mind, through the knowledge of the love of Christ, was a wonderfully liberating force. A blending of the cultural and spiritual within our perception of Christ as spiritual and physical liberator in our lives is further exemplified by the more than three hundred slave rebellions that history records, most of which were led by ministers.[19] Our modern views of Christ as liberator resulted primarily from the political and social gains from which we have benefited from the 1950s onward. Christ spoke of the need to treat one another well and noted that doing for others was doing for him (Matthew 25:40).

Brown v. the Board of Education, the civil rights movement, the women's movement, the movement against environmental racism, community economic development efforts, and targeted health improvements for racial minority groups have each led in distinct ways to our capacity to make individual and group advancements in our lives. As a result, our educational, employment, residential, life expectancy, and social opportunities have greatly improved, though not nearly enough. Additionally, as we have had the benefit of these advancements—through Christ's liberation on a social level—we have lost many advancements through the same political processes by which we gained them, and in some cases, through our own behavior (viewing education as a *white* achievement, as an example).

Once freed from sin, we may choose not to sin. Making the choice not to sin is a choice to understand that African Americans who are Christian have three forms of liberation that influence our lives— Christ's liberty, ancestral liberty, and American liberty. While Christ's sacrifice for us should be sufficient to make us sin-free, we know that the world's temptations make this a challenge for many of us. An examination of the liberties available to us may make easier the choice to set sin aside:

Christ's liberty. "God sent not his Son into the world to condemn the world; but that the world through him might be saved" (John 3:17, KJV). This is the very definition of Christian liberty.

Ancestral liberty. Those who died in the Middle Passage, bled under the slave master's whip, worked to pass civil rights legislation, marched on Washington, and became elected officials in government, have provided not just for African Americans, but for all Americans, access to freedoms that are models for the democracy in the world.[20]

American liberty. The experiment of American democracy, though clearly not perfect in its execution, provides recourse through the media, the legislative and executive branches of government, and the streets, and has given African Americans a source of power and liberty that cannot be taken for granted.

The convergence of these liberties—Christian, ancestral, and American—should provide all of us with an awareness of the sacrifices that have been made for us. Once aware of those sacrifices, we should be much more aware that the option of sin, though the opportunity is all around us, is an opportunity that denigrates those important sacrifices. It also degrades the importance of the life we have been given and the legacy we engage as we live it.

Perhaps because I was the child of a minister, as a very young girl I became interested in obituaries and the sociology of cemeteries.[21] My interest was not morbid; instead, I was aware that I was learning about the entirety of a person's life. Since that time, when people make certain decisions, such as creating or perpetuating conflicts, it is clear to me that they are writing their epitaphs. When we act as an acknowledgment of the liberties we have been given through the sacrifices, first of Christ, then of many others, our epitaphs should be clearly in our sights.

Core Value: Liberty lives in personal and spiritual choice.[22]

THE BALM OF THE HOLY SPIRIT

"God is spirit, and those who worship him must worship in spirit and in truth." (John 4:24, NRSV)

There is a balm in Gilead
To make the wounded whole;
There is a balm in Gilead
To heal the sin-sick soul.[23]

The faith of our fathers, as passed down to us, has been strengthened and fortified by an absolute and abiding faith in a triune God, as Father, Son, and Holy Ghost. These three aspects to our one God are an indication, according to the scholar Samuel K. Roberts, that God is essentially spiritual. "It is absolutely clear that if God is to be God, then God must transcend matter, not be contingent upon matter, and therefore be beyond matter."[24] The Holy Spirit, defined as distinct from the Father and Son, yet completely God,[25] is believed to have guided prophets and kings since before Christ's arrival on earth, to be the force of locution behind those blessed to speak in tongues (see Acts 2:4), and to have descended on Christ during his baptism (see John 1:29-34).

John, among the other gospel writers, focused on describing the role of the Holy Spirit within the context of Christ's ministry. John wrote that we are baptized by the Holy Spirit, viewing water as a transformative force that washes away our sins and renews us as new souls in Christ (John 1:29-33), that the Holy Spirit gives spiritual life (John 6:63), and that Christ gives the Holy Spirit to those who believe in him (John 7:38-39). Jesus also taught his disciples about the Holy Spirit in the Upper Room, foreshadowing his death as well as describing the role that the Holy Spirit would play as an Advocate and Comforter (John 16:7), one who would dwell only in believers (John 14:17), and as a balm to our wounds, a comforting and enduring gift from God (John 14:16).

Core Value: There is a balm in Gilead to make the wounded whole.

THE POWER OF THE HOLY SPIRIT

Christian faith would be severely impoverished were it not for a belief in the power and efficacy of the Holy Spirit. Just as the Christian faith would not be recognizable as a faith system without the belief that through God's grace Jesus of Nazareth became the Christ of faith, so also would that faith be something quite different were it not for a belief in the Holy Spirit. Adolf Holl, a German Catholic scholar, has boldly declared that, without the Holy Spirit, Jesus never would have become Christ and the religion that traces itself to Jesus Christ would have had to look for another name.[26]

For African Americans, the Holy Spirit serves as a spiritual and life force by acting in three distinct ways:

Christian purpose. We are baptized into the faith in the presence of the Holy Spirit[27] and call on the Holy Spirit in times of spiritual need, seeking the balm that Christ has made available to us. We seek this balm both for prayers of petition and intercession.

Historical African American role. "When God speaks to me now in the Spirit, I move and move with certainty," said a slave when asked to describe the Holy Spirit's impact on his sojourn through life.[28] The bridges that brought us over include the intercessory prayers of such elders. Those prayers and experiences of the Holy Spirit, still present in the universe, comfort and envelope us. In addition, because we have heard about the strength and comforting force of the Holy Spirit in the lives of the ancestors and our living elders, we have a mighty trust, in addition to Christ's promise, in what it will do for us, even when we are unaware that we need its power.

Modern role. When we pray, sing, dance for the Lord, or raise holy hands, we are invoking the Holy Spirit to enter our hearts and, through its presence there, to have a meaningful impact on our lives. That effect, often dichotomous, can be simultaneously calming, energizing, consoling, and reassuring, and, for each person, deeply personal, whether it occurs in privacy or is shared in the experience of corporate worship.

The Holy Spirit transcends the time and space of historically Christian, African American ancestral, and intensely personal spiritual experiences. Understanding the Holy Spirit in its many historical and modern manifestations is essential to finding a place of comfort with which it can nestle into each life. It is easy to objectify the Holy Spirit as words that we say or sing, but it is much more difficult to truly comprehend it as a component of Christ, a protective balm for our souls, and the key by which we gain everlasting life.

Core Value: The Holy Spirit helps us cradle the entirety of our ancestral, familial, societal, and personal experiences, as together these things comprise who we are and why we require prayer, support, love, and redemption.

ROCK OF OUR SALVATION
I go to the rock of my salvation
I go to the stone that the builders rejected
Run to the mountain and the mountain stands by me
When all around me is sinking sand
On Christ the solid rock I stand
When I need a shelter, when I need a friend
I go to the Rock
—Words and Music by Dottie Rambo[29]

Christ has many names—Mighty Counselor, Lord of Lords, and Prince of Peace. But among them is not so much a name but the concept that Jesus provides for us a solid and strong place of refuge and sanctuary when the world (or ourselves in the world) becomes unsafe: the idea that Jesus is our Rock. Christ is the Rock of our salvation and our Rock in a weary land.

Jesus has our backs! When we are unable to stand on our own, Christ lifts us up, pulls us out of our doldrums, and reminds us that we are his. We are promised little in this life but grace and, in this, as in all else, Jesus surrounds us with his love.

As is stated in the hymn *Amazing Grace*, as is lived in our history, and as must be taught to our children to sustain us, "through many dangers, toils and snares, we have already come."[30] Our faith gives us stability, and Christ is the bedrock of our faith.

Core Value: Though Christ is ever our Rock, he has also given us the strength individually and as a community to be our own rock(s).

next steps

Conflict always occurs in a context that is much larger than the issue that the conflict addresses or than is immediately apparent to those engaged in it. Conflicts can be positive, growth-producing, and ultimately redemptive if parties understand that church conflicts are often a matter of differing perspectives; the goal is for the relationship to heal and grow rather than for one person or group to win; and skills can be developed to make conflicts as creative and productive as possible.[31]

Our core beliefs, ethical lessons, and core values should, when taken together, act as spiritual knowledge and protection from significant, antagonistic, church-splitting, and soul-rending conflict. Because the causes of conflict are larger than the obvious and hidden issues that underlie them, and because, in fact, the church grows from the presence of conflicts that are well-managed, the humanity of conflict cannot easily be avoided. Within that humanity, however, we must also strive to clearly understand the values that guide our behavior.

We know well how to help people in need. Recall how we rallied after the attacks of September 11, 2001. We took strangers into our homes, fed one another, collected funds for those who had lost loved ones, supported first responders,[32] and returned to places of worship in droves, seeking answers for our confused spirits and broken hearts. As heartfelt as all of these efforts may have been, these collective contributions, made on irregular bases, are things we not only can do but, more importantly, agree should be done.

Ethical issues are a bit trickier. They are areas in which conflict is inherently born. After all, we can agree that we should help those who have needs, but we cannot always agree on who those people are and how we should help them. That said, ultimately it may be more important to change the nature of our conflicts from arguing over who has moral values or whose values and ethics are more valid to determining how to build a Christian community based on workable compromises with shared goals and dreams.

3

anger in perspective

As God's anger is of short duration, so should ours be.
As God does not nurse anger, neither should we. As
God is gracious and compassionate, so must we be. As Jesus
understood all that his tradition said about God in the light
of these absolutely primary affirmations, so should we.[1]

ASK THE AVERAGE PERSON TO DESCRIBE WHAT HE OR SHE EXPECTS
to find on entering the building known as church and the
answer most give will likely have something to do with an
expectation of a sense of peace. *Calm, quiet, serenity, silence, tranquility, harmony,* and *sanctuary* are among the words used to describe
what people expect to feel in God's house. Our lives outside the church
are often in turmoil; we come to church seeking God's peace. While we
bring with us the joy in our hearts, burnished by our love of Christ, we
also bring with us our many hurts, wounds, and needs, and ask God
to heal them. Ironically, it is exactly because of these needs that church
is frequently not the peaceful place we would like it to be. In fact, often
the sanctuary is most calm, quiet, and serene when we are not in it!

While it is good to desire a sense of peace and calm, we do well to
understand that our capacity for emotion—the full range from joy to
pain—is ultimately and most certainly a gift from God. If we have no
experience of one emotional extreme, we cannot fully understand or
appreciate the other.

Physical pain teaches other lessons, as well. People who suffer from the
rare genetic disorder Congenital Pain Insensitivity with Analgesia (CPIA)
are unable to feel any pain at all. This inability to feel pain predisposes

this group of people to serious difficulties in functioning, some of which can be fatal. The experience of physical, social, and emotional pain is a signal to us that something is wrong that requires our attention.

This same dynamic applies to the experience of anger, which of course is closely associated with conflict. Addressing conflict in healthy ways requires that we accept and understand anger, as opposed to denying it or running from it. There are two different kinds of anger in the pews: the sort that is basically healthy (approximately 95–99 percent); and antagonistic anger (occurring among 1–5 percent of members).[2]

Generally speaking, "antagonists" in this context are individuals who, on the basis of nonsubstantive evidence, go out of their way to make insatiable demands, usually attacking the person or performance of others. These attacks are selfish in nature. They tear down rather than build up and are frequently directed against those in a leadership capacity.[3]

Malevolent in their intent, antagonists are frequently emotionally ill persons who create conflict because they have personality or character disorders.[4] In some cases, they may address valid issues, but they address these issues inappropriately as a result of their illnesses or personalities. Those who feel abused by antagonizing church members need to make the proper mental health referrals through church ministries or community agencies. We must all remember Christ's words that "in the world you will have tribulation" (see John 16:33) and to "pray for those who mistreat you" (see Luke 6:28).

Let's turn to some positive features of anger. According to Leroy Howe, author of *Angry People in the Pews: Managing Anger in the Church*, there are three positive components to the anger felt by those in the pew if it can be successfully managed.

> [T]he capacity to feel anger at all is one of God's most precious gifts to us, and therefore...getting angry is a normal and predictable part of our experience and growth as God's creatures. The second point is that though anger sometimes gets out of

hand there is always power available to us for overcoming its excesses and for restoring whatever relationship(s) may be threatened by them. The power is in the Holy Spirit, bearing witness to what our Lord Jesus teaches all of his followers, then and now, about the proper role of anger in both divine and human life. The third major point...is that God calls each of us to draw upon this power and this teaching, first to better deal with our own anger, and then to help our brothers and our sisters in the faith deal better with theirs. When all followers of Christ finally accept this call and seek to fulfill it faithfully in their own lives, then we will be close to the day when the congregations of which we are a part become the havens of peace for which we so fervently long.[5]

Anger, then, is but one type of psychic pain that can signal the potential for conflicts that might occur in our churches. It is also one of God's necessary gifts to us, one that assists us in recognizing that change may be needed for the sake of ourselves, our brothers and sisters, and the greater community.

biblical anger

God the Father and Christ the Son had moments of anger. Unlike most of the human anger or other emotions that lead to our negatively caused conflict, God's anger and Christ's anger are purposeful and for just cause. Their anger was designed to teach lessons about the role of God and our Savior as sole heads of our lives. The plagues of the Old Testament were signs of God's anger, indicating his pique when he was not sufficiently honored by the people of Israel. God indicated in other instances that he would not tolerate the worship of false idols (see Deuteronomy 32:21) or hearts turned away from a God who had treated his people with great favor (see Hosea 13). Carrying these lessons on in a New Testament example, when Christ drove the money changers out of the temple (see Matthew 21:12-13), he was teaching the importance of reverence for God's house.

These examples of anger had a specific purpose: to teach. Divine anger does not ever lead to conflict. Instead, it causes the human beings toward whom it is directed to stop, to reflect, to redirect their efforts, and, hopefully, to prayerfully make the behavioral changes necessary to do what God wants.

Divine anger, then, differs significantly in form and function from the human range of emotions that can, and frequently do, create conflict in all avenues of our lives.

anger in a polarized society

The emotion of anger has become more prominent with the polarization of our society. Increasingly, as attested to by many research groups, media outlets, and denominational leaders, we are a country, and, in many cases, a people of faith, divided. The church has some of its conflicts because the church is a reflection of the conflicts that exist in the world. This cannot be what God wants. The faithful of God attend church, actively participate in Bible study, quote Scripture, and pray fervently, but we do not get along.

Civil society is dying; we have to a large extent forgotten how to get along. It is hypothesized that the lack of community partly explains the challenges we face interacting successfully, being patient with one another, and engaging in basic civility. The social structures that help us create community are increasingly rare in American society. Homes rarely have porches these days, places where people sit, greet neighbors, and can see what is happening in their communities. People live in apartment buildings for years without ever meeting or greeting their neighbors. The "neighborhood" is now the computer "chat room," an impersonal technological place, but one that allows people to create disconnected relationships, many of which, without the benefit of true personal contact, are false and potentially dangerous. There is no longer the communal marketplace—the town square—of the 1950s and 1960s.[6] Though those years had certain obvious racial disadvantages for black Americans, people knew one another and could count on one another for support. Economically disadvantaged black children could see the doctor or the teacher who lived down the street, dream, and plan constructively for their own futures.

Our national dependence on cell phones has also, ironically, aided our personal disconnection from one another by creating an environment in which we no longer know how to be alone. We are connected to one another at the ear, constantly calling, text messaging, and talking because we are afraid of what may occur if we are left alone with our solitude.

This lack of connectedness is both reflected by and caused by how people view church. Barna states that an increasing number of Americans, though steeped in their faith, are beginning to view their churches as "rest stops" along their spiritual paths, rather than final destinations.[7] There is a considerable degree of "church hopping," in which congregants make decisions on which church to go to based on where certain choirs sing on a particular Sunday or on where the pastor with the fiery preaching style can be heard. They never become members of any congregation.

> The "rest stop" phenomenon is fueled, says Barna, by four main factors:
>
> Our transience—15 to 20 percent of all households relocate each year;
>
> Our preference for variety in our church experiences, rather than getting the most that a single church has to offer;
>
> Our perception that spiritual enlightenment comes from diligence in a discovery process, rather than commitment to a faith group and perspective; and
>
> Our repositioning of religion as a commodity that we consume, rather than one in which we invest ourselves.[8]

The good news is that the church has the opportunity to model for our society a different way of processing anger and addressing conflict. It is to this topic that we now turn our attention.

4
principles and perspectives for managing conflict

There's not a liberal America and a conservative America—there's the United States of America. There's not a black America and white America and Latino America and Asian America; there's the United States of America. The pundits like to slice-and-dice our country into Red States and Blue States; Red States for Republicans, Blue States for Democrats. But I've got news for them, too. We worship an awesome God in the Blue States, and we don't like federal agents poking around our libraries in the Red States. We coach Little League in the Blue States and have gay friends in the Red States. There are patriots who opposed the war in Iraq and patriots who supported it.[1]

WITH THE ABOVE WORDS, PART OF HIS KEYNOTE ADDRESS DURing the Democratic Convention in the summer of 2004, Barack Obama, the first African American senator from Illinois, may have said it best. His speech tapped into the country's confusion, conflict, and anger, while trying to hold out the mantle of hope and reconciliation to a nation that feels, to many, to be divided.

Senator Obama knew that, in addressing "hot topics" such as homosexuality and the war in Iraq, he would push some buttons. Not everyone is comfortable talking about these topics, and we have lost some of our capacity for civility in conversation. "We can disagree," Mr. Obama says in all of his public appearances, "without being disagreeable."

One of the skills that allowed Senator Obama to create consistent political wins "across the aisle" for state senatorial office in Illinois and to become the third black senator in Congress since Reconstruction is his affable ability to disagree without being disagreeable. In winning through this tactic, Mr. Obama set a remarkable example for us and quietly issued a challenge to our community. The challenge was one that was taught by our parents and practiced in our schoolyards. It was simply this: "We needn't like each other, but we must respect each other." Seeing the humanity in others requires that we get along. Or, as my maternal grandmother, Laura Jones, often put it, "You can see God in the eyes of his children."[2] When you realize that God is who you are looking at and talking to, it should change the nature of the conversation.

The important point of Mr. Obama's keynote speech was that, wherever we live, whoever we are, we are loved by God regardless. And so are our neighbors loved by God, regardless of their views on divisive topics, or what politicians say about them, or what the people down the block might think. What a wonderful challenge it is to love our neighbors as God loves them. Our hearts, if we let them, are capable of changing.

According to Eddy Hall, an expert in the management of church conflict, conflict is a prerequisite for the development of real intimacy.[3] Churches that can learn to manage their love-based conflict, and even that limited amount that the devil drags in, will be better equipped to engage their ministries effectively. Conflict should never be avoided, which is not fully possible anyway. Ultimately, churches that deal with conflict directly are healthier than those that run from it.

conflicts affecting the church

While those who sit in the pews come into the church with personal conflicts as well as those fueled by the broader social environment, the congregation is the best source for determining what conflicts affect the church. People in the pews teach the pastor, church leaders, one another, and, in some instances, the external community, about some of the most important issues that face the church and what church members feel about them.

As detailed in *View from the Pew: What Preachers Can Learn from Church Members*, the issues of most concern to congregation members focused on a number of behaviors targeted at creating pastoral excellence. Because these were not always behaviors that pastors were likely to admit to themselves—and because those who sit in the pew often have no way of communicating their concerns to their pastors directly—there was potential for significant, but unspoken, conflict.

To diminish the possibility for conflict, congregants wanted their pastors to:

> *Be prepared to preach*. Preachers should be trained so that they can adequately teach and preach the Word of God, and must never enter the pulpit without being properly prepared.
>
> *Celebrate the centrality of Christ*. Preachers should "preach to the coasts,"[4] recognizing that, while they have a special call, they are, nonetheless, one with those who sit in the pews. Additionally, it is important not to limit the size of God's house or their ministries by preaching to the "church," believing that the building is where God's work is done. The church exists outside of the walls of the building in which we worship, and we must be encouraged to do God's work in the church and in the world. When churches are too insular, a church form of groupthink can occur. That form of insularity breeds the possibility of conflict.
>
> *Preach God's words, not your words*. Preachers must be cautious and prayerful to preach sermons whose words come from the Lord. The pew recognizes preacher-hubris. This type of pastoral ego creates a distance between pastor and pew that can make it difficult to get the work of the church done, leading to unnecessary conflicts that stem indirectly from the pulpit.
>
> *Be a shepherd, not a showman*. The pew wants preachers who will get out of God's way and who will, despite all of the temptations of this media age, be humble shepherds of God. The perception of showman preachers creates a lack of trust that can feed potential avenues for conflict.

Do the vision thing. Being focused and strategic in the ministry is essential to those who lead our churches. Those in the pew become concerned when they feel that preachers are more concerned about the preaching moment than about excellent and visionary church management, of which preaching is a vital component.

Expose the pastor in you. Because of the many needs that those in the pew bring to the church, having preachers who are also pastoral is essential. Earning the trust of the pew, sharing personal moments through preaching, and connecting with church members in special ways helps decrease the potential for conflict.

Connect the head and the heart. Congregants need preachers to assist them in meeting the many spiritual needs that they bring into the sanctuary. As a place where relationships form and are fed, the preacher serves as a model for how good relationships develop. This model is essential for diminishing conflict and for establishing healthy relationships.

Stand on the shoulders of the saints. According to many of those in the pew, there is too little attention paid to our elders. The pulpit is an excellent place to model that the importance of our ancestors, pastoral and other mentors, and those who influence our community is vital and essential. The continual reminder of what can be learned from these persons creates a pride in self that eliminates our very human tendencies to create drama. When we feel good about ourselves, we work together more effectively and have little need to attempt to feel better at another's expense.

View themselves from the pew. Know that, warts and all, members of the congregation love and care about their pastors and want the best for them. If we see their humanity and caring, they will always have congregational support.

Be satisfied. Preachers must model the best for their congregants and know, at the end, that God is the final judge of their work on earth.[5]

considering the motive

Managing conflict in the church begins with an acknowledgment that most conflict starts from a love for Christ and for Christ's church. When Sister Sally kicks up a fuss over church robes, there are certainly some underlying personal issues that cause her to do so, but beneath even those is a wish for the choir to look good on Sunday mornings so that when they sing, God is truly glorified. When Deacon Jones fights in an unfair manner to secure the chairmanship of the deacon board, it has a lot to do with hubris, but it also has to do with the knowledge that he actually has better managerial skills than Deacon Brown, and a well-run church best brings honor to Christ. Sister Sally and Deacon Jones each enacted their work for Christ in the wrong ways, but their original intentions reflect their good hearts.

thinking things through

At the 2004 commencement of Harvard University, President Lawrence H. Summers discussed the grand stage on which conflicts can occur, as well as the dire consequences that might result if, through the negligence inherent in our humanity, we let history repeat itself. Addressing college seniors in his baccalaureate message, Summers instructed:

> Thinking things through means analyzing them carefully. It also means understanding not just your own perspectives, but also perspectives that threaten your own. Take as an example some of the most fateful decisions made by human beings, decisions about war and peace, decisions like the British failure to understand Hitler at Munich, or the American failure to understand what was and what was not at stake at Vietnam. Millions of people died, not at root because of moral failures but because of intellectual failures of comprehension, failures brought on by weak analysis that overlooked the perspective of the adversary.[6]

Perhaps the most important statement Dr. Summers made reflects an egregious error engaged in by all of those he mentioned: the potentially fateful decision of not understanding or analyzing perspectives that threaten our own. This, of course, is where we get into the most trouble.

This is what caused the backlash—the "How dare you!"—against Bill Cosby over his statements discussed in chapter 2. Perhaps Mr. Cosby's perspective does have some flaws. What was especially surprising, though, was how many people, who in other circumstances would have analyzed all aspects of a problem carefully, simply threw his arguments out on their face.

We do this frequently when we hear perspectives we don't like, perspectives that come from "the other." If we are Democrats, we may dismiss a Republican viewpoint out of hand, and vice versa. When we do so, we miss an opportunity not just to learn from one another but also to engage in important compromise that moves us toward one another. Because we tend to get stuck in a mind-set, we miss the chance to hear an idea we would not have thought of on our own.

People might dismiss viewpoints of persons of other races or ethnicities, even when they grew up with those persons as friends. Positions of relative privilege sometimes cause this to happen without our even stopping to ask the questions that would prevent the process that erode the rights and privileges of those with whom we otherwise share our lives. We sometimes dismiss others' viewpoints because of assumptions about these positions and the roles—both others' and our own—that result from these positions.

Men have for generations underestimated women, while women can make wrong assumptions about the motivations and behaviors of men. All of this misunderstanding may occur based on what may have begun as cultural stereotypes and has extended into our lives because we have not done as Dr. Summers has asked us to do, which is to use the skill of analyzing to do something very difficult: step well outside the zone of our patterns and preferences to understand that which threatens us the most. Doing this requires more than an understanding of the other. It also requires a self-knowledge and capacity for humility. We have to be willing to admit that we have been wrong, both about ourselves and others.

In the case of Mr. Cosby, what was so interesting was that responses so often reserved for "the other" were turned on one of our most illustrious own. Was this done because those of us who are poor turned him into a "rich other"? Was it because Mr. Cosby's words were inelegant and, perhaps, unkind, even though he may have been telling agreed-upon truths? Or was it because some members of the African American community became embarrassed because influential whites heard and publicly reported and discussed what have tended to be private conversations? It is interesting to consider whether or not we have been embarrassed that whites have seen the behavior for years. If that is the case, then why shoot the messenger, especially since he may be saying something that we have said ourselves?

The point of all of this is that African Americans would do well to address Dr. Summers's admonition that we clearly analyze perspectives that threaten our personal status quos. In this case, it means taking into account not just what we think and are afraid of, but also the fears (and conversely, the hopes and dreams) of an entire community. Whatever the effect of Bill Cosby's actions, when we have such discussions in our communities, our homes, and our churches, our methods for dealing with them must reflect that Christ is part of the contract for managing whatever conflict might ensue.

conflict from three perspectives

There are three potential perspectives on how conflict may best be managed in the church, understanding that it begins, almost inevitably (the 90–95 percent), from a place of love.

Pastoral perspective on conflict management. As the head of the local church, the pastor is the primary person expected to manage conflict. The pastoral perspective must be to ask the following questions or to engage in the following behaviors:

1. In the midst of this conflict, how can I care for the souls involved? Because one of the strengths of the black church is that it "serves as a station of personal affirmation which attracts large numbers of persons,"[7] during times of significant church conflict, a focus on pastoral care is very important for those involved.

2. What aspects of this conflict may ultimately be redemptive for those involved? One must have no preconceptions about the individuals or groups involved in the conflict. As pastors create relationships with parishioners, it may be a challenge to put pastoral feelings aside while objectively assessing the issues involved in the conflict. Nonetheless, it is important to be as objective as possible or to, when possible, assign the task of direct conflict management or other intervention to a ministerial or administrative staff member.

3. What tools of the ministry can I use to address the conflict? For example, the pastor might find a Scripture passage that can be used in a sermon as a tool to address the conflict and engage the congregation in the conflict abatement effort. As is stated in *Church Administration in the Black Perspective*, a "preacher is forced to 'pastor from the pulpit.' …Worship is essential for building the base for meaningful church administration."[8]

4. Is my behavior in any way contributing to the conflict? If so, how? Understand that leaders must confess their digressions first. This is never easy but it is the best and most respected model of leadership.[9]

5. What should my prayers be for forgiveness for contributing to the conflict? With whom must I make amends? To whom must I apologize? (Having prayed for forgiveness and apologized to those individuals or groups with whom a pastor has been in conflict, it is important for the pastor to forgive himself or herself for being human in how he or she leads the church and community.)

6. What are my expectations for the outcome? Pastors who responded to a recent national survey conducted by *Leadership Magazine* indicated that 95 percent had experienced conflict, 85 percent cited issues of control as the factor fueling the conflict, and 94 percent expected good outcomes from their experiences with church conflict.[10]

Lay leadership perspective on conflict management. The perspective of lay leaders (deacons, deaconesses, elders, departments heads, and staff members with important task responsibilities) must be to ask the following questions or to engage in the following behaviors:

1. How do I support church and pastoral policy on the remediation of conflicts that occur in the church?

2. How do I best model conflict resolution to the congregation?

3. Is my behavior contributing in any way to the conflict? If so, how? Following the model of the pastor, leaders must confess their digressions first.[11]

4. What should my prayers be for forgiveness for contributing to the conflict? With whom must I make amends? To whom must I apologize? (Having prayed for forgiveness and apologized to those individuals or groups with whom leaders have been in conflicts, leaders must now forgive themselves for being human in their leadership of the congregation and community.)

Congregational perspective on conflict management. The perspective of members of the congregation must be to ask the following questions or to engage in the following behaviors:

1. In what ways am I contributing to the growth of the church through engaging the Great Commission (see Matthew 28:19-20)?

2. In what ways am I using the gifts that God has given me by involving myself actively in my church's groups, committees, activities, organizations, and community outreach opportunities?

3. Am I sharing the needs of families, community members, those in my profession, and the church ministries in which I am involved? Or am I presenting and representing the perspective of the pew as only I know it?

4. Is my behavior in any of these activities contributing in any way to conflicts in my church? If so, how?

5. What should my prayers be for forgiveness for contributing to conflict? With whom must I make amends? To whom must I apologize? (Having prayed for forgiveness and apologized to those individuals or groups with whom they have been in conflict, members must

now forgive themselves for being human and know that forgiveness is a wonderful lesson to family, friends, and oneself.)

Pastors, lay leaders, and members all must share a sense of responsibility for their own behavior. Simply knowing that conflict may begin in love is no reason to start it and every reason to try to get it under control. Knowing that in most cases love is the genesis of conflict, however, increases understanding so that the response to seeing situations of conflict is not anger or bitterness but insight and prayer.

getting past it

We must recognize that most anger has its origins in topics and issues that may have begun in our personal lives and homes. If, for example, we have tended to have difficulty with authority figures in our lives and the chairperson of the missions committee is someone with an authoritarian personality, then conflict is possible and perhaps even likely.

It is a psychological maxim that problems tend to begin for one reason and to continue for another. For example, the authoritarian person with whom we had problems in the past may have been a parent who exercised unreasonable control over our childhood household. Children, obviously, have no control over their parenting. When children become adults, however, control is entirely within their purview. A child may well have lived his or her life acting out against the specter of an authoritative parent, represented by a person or persons in authority over him or her. The primary conflict had to do with anger at a parent, and then, many years later, was made worse when the missions chairperson, who may indeed have been unreasonable, acted in a manner reminiscent of the parent. Because the adult who grew up in the authoritative household never developed the skills needed to deal with anger and to manage conflicts in reasonable ways, there will likely be problems, perhaps in a marriage, at work, with parenting, or with the chairperson of the missions committee.

There will, in fact, be problems that arise in the church itself that are ample fodder for the division of established groups, for backstabbing and backbiting, and for all kinds of ugly and ungodly behavior. The ways that we handle the conflicts that arise naturally will, nonetheless, be based on what we have learned in our life histories, how we interact based on friendships and alliances that have been formed both inside and outside the church, and what pushes our buttons when we are stressed. Thus it is essential for each of us to use our relationships with God and the resources that he has made available to us (including therapy, the Bible, and prayer) to work through the issues from the past. We have to get past our pasts to effectively move beyond the conflicts that we may create in our lives, including in the church.

playing by the rules

In every church, the pastor and church leadership are likely to have developed written policies about how to manage significant conflicts of the type that may have to lead to asking members to leave their positions on committees. Church members should, as a component of their membership, become familiar with church policies. Through information passed to congregations in sermons, Bible study, and other church activities, members will have learned rules about expected behaviors. Rules, however, cannot prevent the church from becoming a hotbed of gossip, turf wars, struggles for power, and other forms of conflict about which rules are not written. Though the Golden Rule should cover this area, human beings forget. Although treating others as we would like to be treated might be less interesting than having something to call each other about when the church meeting is over, it is the behavior that God expects of us.

Consider that conflict reflects love in the pews and opportunity in the wings. One of the opportunities is for our relationship with Christ to deepen. Conflict is a "primary means of sanctification: It's not something we go looking for, but when it comes, we slow down and say, 'Lord, if nothing else in this situation, refine me.'"[12]

the 8 p's: 8 strategies for managing conflict

> Let the church roll on.
> Let the church roll on.
> Oh Lord, let the church roll on.
>
> There's a sister in the church
> And her skirt's too short.
> Tell me what you gonna do?
> Take some scissors, cut the hem!
> And let the church roll on!
>
> There's a preacher in the church
> And he cuss too much.
> Tell me what you gonna do?
> Take the Bible, kick him out!
> And let the church roll on!
>
> So let the church roll on![1]

THIS SONG IS, OF COURSE, A TONGUE-IN-CHEEK ACCOUNT OF EVENTS that have actually been witnessed in African American churches. The responses to these events are ways of trying to deal with problems raised by difficult behaviors.

We have learned that the quest to arrive at "Amen moments" in our churches—to move from chaos to genuine Christian community—requires that we become committed to understanding the nature of conflicts. We know—or at least we should know—that the church does not advance through holy wars, whether they are writ large on the global scale or occur as a result of personal skirmishes in the church office. We have learned that, as part of the body of Christ committed to working together to heal its wounds, we must admit that we, too, are wounded in body and spirit. What we cannot consciously do, in spite of personal wounds, is be the administrators of wounds to others. Getting to Amen, then, requires that we know the rules of conflict so that we can manage it constructively and fairly.

With the 8 P's, I offer an Afri-Christian model consisting of eight related but distinct strategies for managing conflict in our churches. It should not be considered an infallible solution, as in "Follow steps one through four and the problem will be solved." Rather, it offers general principles that can be applied more specifically based on each individual arena of conflict.

THE 8 P'S

Prayer—When the pain that causes rifts is in God's house, the first step on the path to healing must be prayer.

Preaching—As the platform from which most parishioners get their information, the sermon can either be a tool for healing or can contribute to divisiveness in the church.

Parishioner Awareness—Church members have a considerable amount of misinformation that contributes to church-related conflicts. Providing correct information, which entails using lay leaders and church officers as ambassadors of detailed and helpful communication, can play key roles in healthy conflict resolution.

Perspective(s) on Problems—Church conflicts result from the different perspectives held by the very human members of God's house. For conflict to be resolved, church members must explore ways to move beyond frozen stances in order to establish common goals.

Practical Solutions—Once common goals are identified, practical solutions are more easily adopted and implemented.

Programs and Premises—Long-term structures can be put in place through the creation of policies designed by all parties and through programs (ministries) based on those policies.

Pastoral Management—Excellent church management leads by example. If the pastor sets a conflict-free example and a well-organized model, the church is more likely to follow his or her lead.

Promises—Promises look toward the future and help churches make plans to maintain their conflict-free structures by coordinating ministries with other local, national, and international church groups that share the goals of strengthening the Afri-Christian diaspora.

The structure of this model is holistic, as are we as a people. Components of the model, some original, are based on my training as a psychologist and on my work in conflict management, including training with the Harvard Negotiation Project and John Paul Lederach's[2] international model of peaceful negotiation, affiliated with the Eastern Mennonite Church, as well as learning derived from serving as an election monitor for the first democratic election in El Salvador.[3] Other aspects of the model draw from available resources, adapted to our style, behaviors, history, and needs.

This holistic model recognizes that we need to move through a process that begins with a recognition that God is great and that, without an acknowledgment of God's greatness and purpose in our lives, getting to Amen will be difficult if not impossible. That is why the first step of the process is always Prayer. The process is designed to push congregations into uncomfortable places in some instances, understanding that to get past conflict between people, it is necessary to create conflict in thought processes. Parishioner Awareness and Perspec-tive(s) on Problems, even Preaching and Pastoral Management, may fall into this category. Congregations are also asked to come up with their own creative ideas about getting past conflict. It is important not just to manage conflict, but in some cases to address the issues that have been problematic in the African American church and community through the development of specific programs. Being proactive is part of what makes this model unique, and Programs and Premises is available for this purpose. Finally, the model ends with Promises because it is essential that, to maintain conflict-free or conflict-neutral environments, churches must look to and strategically plan for the future. Getting to Amen is supposed to be a glorious and not a grueling process. The 8 P's is a hands-on model that we can use and make our own in addressing the topics that have so often been divisive and painful for us.

Following is a more detailed discussion of each of the 8 P's.

prayer

The first step on the path to healing must be prayer. In each topical chapter that follows, this section will either suggest or present a prayer or a prayer activity. These prayers and activities, whether traditional or nontraditional, will ask readers to engage in petitioners and intercessory prayers. It is essential that we look within ourselves before we pray, that we pray for ourselves to address how we might have contributed to any potential conflict, that we pray for those involved in the conflicts and how they might feel as a result of how we have behaved toward them, that we pray for the resolution of their role in the conflict, and that through God's help the conflict will be resolved so that the work of the church can roll on.

preaching

We do not like to think of our pastors as being divisive, though people in the pews all have stories about circumstances when, from the pulpit or behind the scenes, the pastor has made a mess of church life and church business. It is essential that pastors remember the importance of their roles as Christ's emissaries and that they behave as models for their parishioners. Preaching can reflect pastors' personal views, certainly, but those views should never be small in scope or mean in purpose. The preaching moment must always lift up the beauty of Christ and the stories of Christ, and the preaching must create opportunities for those in the congregation to feel welcomed, to want to join with the body of Christian believers rather than run screaming from it.

parishioner awareness

Ethicist Dr. Bruce Weinstein has a model that is an excellent starting point for those involved in church conflict. It is based on his book *What Should I Do? 4 Simple Steps to Making Better Decisions in Everyday Life*. Dr. Weinstein cautions that it is essential to get information about the issue of importance in addition to thinking about personal values as a way of problem solving. Dr. Weinstein's four-step process for working through any decision-making process in which an ethical decision is required consists of the following basic steps:[4]

Gather the relevant facts. In a church setting, those facts are going to include finding out the basic "w" questions (who, what, when, where, why, and sometimes how). In all cases, our assumptions about what has caused the conflict will shift as we gain answers to our questions. (Sometimes not all questions will be answered. That must be accepted, as insisting that all questions be answered can create a whole new category of conflict.)

Identify the values at stake. What values, personal or Christian,[5] are in conflict? It may be that the conflict is over facts and not values, which provides both sides some bargaining chips for solving the problems.

Consider the options. Once questions have been asked (and answered) and important values identified, it is time to determine what kinds of options and opportunities are available for solving the problem or problems that an individual or congregation faces.

Consider the best option. With any set of options, in considering the timing of the conflict, the context in which it occurs, the personalities of those involved, the values in play, and the nature of the issue, one option among those available will usually appear to be the best. With the agreement of those involved, it should be adopted and eagerly implemented with none of the other options brought up again.

perspective(s) on problems

The Japanese moviemaker Akira Kurosawa made the classic film *Ran*, in which a murder is seen from the perspectives of three protagonists.[6] This approach, unusual when the film was screened in 1985, reminds pastors, church leaders, and parishioners that church conflicts easily result from the different perspectives held by the very human members of God's house. So that church members can move beyond impenetrable ideas and immovable viewpoints to see their common goals, it is important to make the effort to view problems from perspectives other than one's own.

On a National Public Radio call-in show, people were asked to describe an important exposure to art in their lives. A mother called in to describe an experience she'd had with her year-old daughter at the Hirschorn Sculpture Garden in the nation's capital. They were looking at a metal sculpture of an animal. Her daughter had crawled underneath it to a place where she could not easily be reached. The mother kept calling her daughter to come out, noticing that the child was lying in the grass on her back, looking up, fascinated. Finally, the mother got under the sculpture as well and realized what held her daughter in such awe. Though the outside appearance of the sculpture was of an animal, from underneath, it was a six-pointed star, opening up into infinity. The mother would not have known that had she not looked. The lesson for her was twofold: she was reminded, she said, first that she must always look for alternative perspectives and, second, that she should sometimes follow unexpected leaders. The church needs to do this as well. Our leadership should not be as static as it is, nor our rules as rigid, or our perspectives as unvaried. It would be good to lie down and look up at the stars to see what surprises and new perspectives God has in store for us.

practical solutions

Once common goals are identified, practical solutions for handling conflict are more easily implemented. The following ABCs of getting to Amen, adapted from Norma Cook Everist's *Church Conflict: From Contention to Collaboration,*7 contain useful perspectives on conflict management in the African American church context.

Avoidance. Conflict, for most people, does not feel good. And so we avoid it. We see Brother Smith coming and know he wants to discuss the business of the finance committee and that it requires a vote that had the group in a contentious meeting until ten o'clock last Wednesday night. So we wave quickly, grab Sister Loreatha's arm, and start adjusting some random girl-child's braids as we make our way to the church door. Avoidance is a short-term nonsolution. You might not have an immediate solution, but direct communication is always best. The example here is, "Brother Smith, I need a little more time to research and think about that issue. I promise to get back to you in two days."

Accommodation. Accommodation has positive and negative connotations depending on what side of the bargaining table your seat is on. Accommodation should never feel like a wholesale giving in to someone more powerful with whom an individual or church group may, for good reasons, disagree ("Okay, Brother Jackson, since you are the representative of the assistant pastor, we will do it your way"). This is negative accommodation. The example at the end of the Avoidance section illustrated positive accommodation. Rather than avoid Brother Smith, Sister Justice made a reasonable accommodation to his needs. By asking for more time to research and think through issues on the finance committee, she demonstrated commitment to the team. By placing her response within a time frame (rather than saying, "I'll get back to you," which is another avoidance tactic), she furthers the accommodation by making a promise that is clearly understood by all involved. Mutual accommodation is a true form of discipleship.

Bartering. Bartering in essence is compromise, meeting another halfway. It entails, of course, giving up something we hold dear. It requires making a decision about our priorities, a task that is exceptionally difficult for any of us. But bartering also offers an opportunity for everyone to have a relatively equal role in contributing to a solution to problems. Churches do, of course, have hierarchies that give some persons and groups more power, but still everyone should have a voice that is heard and acknowledged. Churches in general find this difficult, and, as a result, they sometimes split. Church splits are not the kind of thing anyone keeps statistics on, though sometimes a split can be inferred from the name of the church. If, for example, a church was named True Vine, the name of the split might be something like Greater True Vine. Today, rather than changing names in this manner, pastors may choose to start a nondenominational church.

Many long-time saints have war wounds resulting from pastors who have come into established congregations and who, determined to make their mark, have tried to force change. The result is people feeling pushed out of the door or a congregation splitting. The alternative, as difficult as it is, is bartering, being willing to give up something we hold dear in order to hold on to something else we hold dear, namely, the unity of the church.

Competition. Though Galatians 5:26 (NRSV) teaches, "Let us not become conceited, competing against one another, envying one another," churches, like the rest of society, are part of a competitive culture. The competition is there, even though we do not always acknowledge it. Black preachers try to "out-hoop" one another; they compete with regard to the numbers in their congregations or how many join on a given Sunday. Hat-wearing church ladies compete over the beauty of their adornments. We even compete over how large our Bibles are, just about breaking our arms with the Word to prove how much we love the Lord! Competition creates clashes in the church; those clashes lead to conflict. The management of that conflict requires the development of trusting relationships in which all voices can be fairly heard. Typically, strategies for addressing competition in the church have included debate, voting, and contests. While these methods can be done in a manner that does not create winners and losers, it is also a good idea to consider the use of approaches that do not engage parishioners in win-lose interactions. Among these tactics are creating congregational conflict-negotiation clinics, teaching young parishioners interpersonal skills, and restructuring language in the church to be noncompetitive through its use in Christian education classes and as modeled in sermons.

Control. It is idolatrous to behave as if we have all power, because that is God's domain. We are tempted to the reins of control, however, because the exercise of power over people and institutions is like an amazing drug. While God has asked us to be stewards over one another and the earth, and while we are certainly expected to be responsible in our positions of authority relative to our families and employment, stewardship and power differ in the manner in which they are engaged. Stewardship implies a covenant relationship with God. Pastors, for example, are presumed to be in positions of power in the church, but if they are doing their jobs well, they are stewards, called of God, with awesome responsibilities as church shepherds with authority over church management. Parishioners often have a certain amount of fear of their pastors that some pastors tend to exploit. This is an unhealthy use of power. Used well, however, control is an effective conflict management technique. It requires understanding when to take and when to relinquish authority, how to develop church leaders, expert ways to shape and move agendas, setting boundaries, and establishing and managing time lines.

Compassion. Compassion is a highly underrated conflict management strategy and tool. Getting to Amen means, in all cases, finding what is human in us, understanding what we share, and, regardless of what may be different, learning to love it. For too short a time September 11, 2001, taught us this lesson. A horrific attack on our country solidified our identity not as disparate groups, but as Americans.[8] On that day, I was stuck in a Los Angeles hotel that had been turned into a staging area for SWAT teams. The first call I received was from a Muslim friend who lived in London and wanted to be assured, since my home was in Washington, D.C., that I was safe. First reaching my parents in Seattle, after not finding me at home, he got my Los Angeles hotel and cell phone numbers. The mosque on his London street was later bombed, and he was subjected to terrible discrimination simply because he wanted to pray for peace. But his compassion on that day looked beyond faith boundaries.

Collaboration. Working together is something that black folks certainly know how to do, though we sometimes run the gamut from being playfully to seriously combative about it. "Collaboration is both a means and a goal; a strategy and a sustainable environment."[9] Collaboration is essential to our capacity to truly live together as a Christian community. African Americans must call upon our faith, our reserves of energy and creativity, to work toward consensus and get past areas of impasse.

programs and premises

Long-term structures can be put in place through the creation of policies designed by all parties. The long-term structures can also be the result of programs (ministries) based on those policies. Such connections ensure that the work all groups have done to move from conflict to creation for Christ and community have lasting results.

pastoral management

Excellent church management leads by example. If the pastor sets a conflict-free or conflict-neutral example and a well-organized model, the church is more likely to follow his or her lead. Interestingly, it may be easiest to think about this form of management through the lens of Christian confrontation, as outlined below.

Understanding your role. As I learned from writing *View from the Pew*, parishioners really watch the pastor and expect that he or she will serve as a model for the congregation. The African American community also expects that pastors will be actively involved with them, assisting them in sorting out social and economic issues. While there are some preachers who don't see this as their role and find biblical justification to maintain a focus on ministry inside the doors of the church, the black community by and large has other expectations. In his ministry, Jesus rarely went into a temple, preferring to minister "on the highways and byways." Churches and communities expect our pastors to be spokespeople, out front on important issues, setting guidelines that we can follow, and upholding values that we think are important. While we are not always going to agree with public pastoral positions, African American community members nonetheless have the expectation that black preachers will address issues of social justice and help solve community conflicts.

Seeing yourself as you are seen. Both the pew and the community are forgiving. However, it is essential that preachers realize how closely they are being observed. A preacher who sits in a bar talking on his cell phone on a late weeknight creates discomfort when he then preaches about appropriate behavior within the context of marriage, as there appears to be a disconnect between his actions and his words. Even though nothing untoward may have occurred, it is essential not to give the appearance of impropriety. It is essential that pastors model appropriate behavior at all times. Inappropriate pastoral behavior is a huge source of church conflict and a contributing factor to congregational splits.

Taking the high road. Robert Frost's poem "The Road Not Taken"[10] discussed the importance of striking out on one's own path, finding there the benefit of the unique and individual perspective. When conflicts become ugly, frequently even gospel mobs rule, and people take much lower roads, roads that instead converge in devilish places. It is essential to keep one's own counsel and to take the high ethical road, so that any conflict is dealt with in a Christian manner. Of course, if one is confronting conflict in a Christian manner, one is never actually alone.

promises

We speak of Christ as "the solid Rock." We resonate with the potential of the balm provided to us by the Rock of Gibraltar. We talk about the commission Christ gave to Peter to become the rock upon which the church eternal could be built. These images of Christ, in their reality and symbolism, provide hope and promise. Promise, in the context of conflict management and resolution, is a way of helping our African American churches, through strategic planning, look to the future by identifying practical tools that solidify the promise of Christ by creating an atmosphere in which his children can behave peaceably, respectfully, and lovingly. Through the development of conflict-free structures, coordinated with other local church ministries, national councils, and international groups with similar goals, the African American church can make manifest the promise for which its foreparents prayed, struggled, fought, bled, and died.

The 8 P's allow readers to move beyond negative conflict to broaden perspectives and to stimulate conversation in the church and among those with whom we have relationships. Getting to Amen means trusting the promises of the ancestors whose courage buoys us, heart and mind. It requires trusting God, who never fails. And it means crossing rivers, those we have known and those we cannot easily imagine.

applying the strategies to issues

6

women in church leadership

"You are the light of the world. A city built on a hill
cannot be hid. No one after lighting a lamp puts it under the
bushel basket, but on the lampstand, and it gives light to all the
house. In the same way, let your light shine before others, so
that they may see your good works and give
glory to your Father in heaven."
—Matthew 5:14-16, NRSV

THE BLACK WOMAN'S ROLE IN THE RELIGIOUS SECTOR HAS VARIED widely throughout history. From our African foremothers' familial, religious, educational, and medical leadership roles to the slave woman's position in black society, to the evolving role of African American women in all societal sectors, including the church—a role that has become central in our postslavery community—women have sought and frequently fought for leadership.

Black women have, of necessity, taken on societal leadership roles. Beth Wolk writes: The societal role of African women has a history of independence and leadership. African women control the marketplace, live in a dual-sex political system, are involved in political campaigns, and perform (as) griots. They also may serve as powerful queens. After the advent of slavery, women continued to be regarded equally by black males. Caretakers of the family, they also worked in the fields along with the black males. It was not until African Americans received their freedom and began mimicking the institutions of the white majority that sexuality became an issue.[1]

The role of women in leadership is a source of conflict in part because of the theological view that the Bible prohibits women to be in authority over men. Regarding this issue, it should be noted that in recent decades the African American church as a whole has moved significantly in the direction of acceptance. That is, Scripture passages once viewed as prohibitive of women in leadership are increasingly being reinterpreted in light of the Bible's broader message of gender inclusiveness.

The conflict in the church, however, goes well beyond different interpretations of Scripture. It is related, in part, to traditions that are increasingly being challenged. More specifically, church leadership is traditionally seen as being male. Men have been in positions of authority in the church, while women, as Wolk puts it, have been "responsible for promoting middle class ideals, providing funding for various programs, and running programs such as schools."[2]

There are important dynamics at work here. Because African American men have been so emasculated by the world outside the church and have typically had so few avenues for power in American society, they have tended to hold quite tightly to their titles and opportunities in the church. After all, the church offers many opportunities that are rich with respect to tradition, history, and community standing. Preacher, elder, pastor, and deacon are all roles to which black men can aspire. Being called "Brother," even at the lowest end of the totem pole, is a high honor on a Sunday if one knows that Monday brings bootlicking, even of a high corporate order.

The role of preacher, of course, is the highest and most coveted role in the church. The preacher is responsible for providing spiritual leadership to the congregation, managing the affairs of the church, building denominational relationships, addressing social ills, and more. It's quite an impressive job description. Since the days of slavery and continuing to this day, many African American men have been drawn to the personal and communal power of the pulpit. Many, since youth, have determined to become preachers. The preaching ministry is an important platform to gain community visibility and to wield influence, not just through sharing Christ's words from the pulpit, but by advancing a social agenda. It is no wonder that, historically, many women who have wished to gain access to the preacher's role have been limited to marrying a preacher, thus becoming a first lady of the church.[3]

African American women who have wanted to preach God's Word have been met with a variety of responses, depending upon their denomination's policies (or absence of them), the receptiveness of their local pastor, the availability of other male and female mentor-pastors, seminary training in their city or regions, the support of their families (particularly their husbands), and their own tenacity and commitment, especially when they are met with rejection because of the forwardness or, in some cases, the perceived inappropriateness (or even audacity) of their desire to preach.

According to Wolk, a writer on religious traditions of the African diaspora,

> [women] do not always hold positions of official power. In the Baptist and Methodist churches, women have their own departments within the church. Often, they function as Evangelists, missionaries, teachers, and choir directors. If they do preach, it is without ordination, and often solely to carry out the work of a deceased husband. This is especially true in many Pentecostal denominations. In some black religious denominations, such as Mt. Sinai Holy Church of America, women can be ordained as elders, a position separate from that of preacher. The House of God allows women preachers, while the Firstborn Church of the Living God separated as a result of the liberal stance. Often black women who wish to preach must open independent churches or enter white denominations.[4]

Female diaconate and elder positions are determined by the local church or denomination. For example, since Baptist churches uphold local church autonomy, a single congregation can determine to ordain women as deacons. (I am, as a result, a deacon in the Metropolitan Baptist Church in Washington, D.C. That role is not transferable, however, since another less liberal congregation, while viewing women as capable, may see them only as deaconesses, mission leaders, or in other traditionally female roles.)

The AME Zion Church was first to ordain women into the ministry. Mary Small was ordained an elder in 1897.[5] In general, however, in African American denominations, women have tended to be relegated to "safe" traditional leadership positions in children's, women's, and mission-related ministries, with only 5 percent of U.S. churches being led by a female senior pastor.[6] While there are clear examples of women in exceptional ministerial roles—Rev. Barbara Harris (first female Anglican bishop, 1998); Rev. Vashti McKenzie (first female AME bishop, 2000); and Rev. Suzan Johnson Cook (first female head of the Hampton University Ministers' Conference, 2004)—they have tended to do well as a result of their own courage and resolve, an understanding of God's call upon their lives, and strategic support from men in the ministry, some of whom supported them against church and denominational tradition. The more traditionally male dominant denominations have tended to be Pentecostal, though increasingly women, elders, or prophetesses (sometimes seen visibly on cable networks) have sought or been given leadership, particularly if they are in the empowered position of being married to the pastor.

black women's self-perception

Black I am, oh! daughters fair!
But my beauty is most rare.
Black indeed appears my skin,
Beauteous, comely, all within.[7]

It would be a mistake to attribute the limitations on women in church leadership exclusively to men. We must understand the internal challenges and limitations women themselves face. The above poem was written by Phillis Wheatley (1753–1784), the first published African American female poet and writer, many of whose works stressed the theme of Christian salvation. She was captured in Senegal, enslaved, and educated in New England.

"The Black Beauty" referenced the black woman in the Song of Solomon; it is most certainly allegorical and metaphorical. What is remarkable about "The Black Beauty" has, interestingly, little to do with its biblical referent or its recognition for publication by a white public during this era. Rather, what makes it special is the poem itself reified. In her world, in spite of a life of degradation, Ms. Wheatley found herself beautiful, stately, and magnificent, not just as a personal self-assessment, but in comparison to those who were her oppressors. Ms. Wheatley's view of herself took particular strength because in her immediate history was a cultural knowledge that white women had been put on their particular pedestals of protection, making slave women fair game for white men. Such access caused many women, already spiritually and physically mutilated by slavery, to further harm themselves. Ms. Wheatley, seeing herself as beautiful within this context was a spirited act of bravery and defiance. However, it is an act not easily or routinely emulated. Look at any church pew on a Sunday morning, and it will be filled with comely African American women who are proud descendants of Phillis Wheatley, but who may not be able to stake their claim to equality and full citizenship as boldly as she did.

the 8 p's

Linguists and psychologists who note how the genders work together have paid attention to differences in the ways that men and women handle conflict. The following steps are adapted from Elizabeth George's *Women's Walk with God: Growing in the Fruit of the Spirit*,[8] which focuses on healing our rifts through caring and kindness:

1. *Caring is a part of kindness.* "I've found prayer to be one sure way to nurture care for those who bring me pain. It's true that if you and I will follow Jesus' instruction to 'pray for those who mistreat you' (Luke 6:28), startling changes will occur in our heart. For

starters, the bond of prayer causes us to be vitally and spiritually involved in the lives of the individuals we pray for. Also, through prayer, God softens *our* heart and mind by softening our harshness and melting our selfishness into concern for others—including our enemies!"

2. *Thinking is part of kindness.* "Another sure sign that we are growing in our concern for people is when we begin to think about others and the conditions of their lives. We'll find ourselves looking at people and thinking, 'What would help her? What would help him? What does he need? What does she need?' We'll find ourselves asking God, 'How can I serve this person? How can I make his or her life easier? How can I touch their life, lift their burden?'"

3. *Kindness is the ability to love people perhaps more than they deserve.* It is to:

■ Pray for your enemies because prayer and hatred cannot coexist.

■ Spend time with God owning up to any ill will you have toward an individual or group of people. Ask for God's help in demonstrating the Spirit's kindness to those people.

■ Ask God to help you become known more as a comforter and less as a confronter.

■ Study Jesus' life for examples of kindness and then follow in his steps, keeping a journal of your progress.

■ Pray for God to fill your heart with his compassion as you walk each day and every step along the way with him.

With care, thoughtfulness, and kindness in mind, let's look now at the 8 P's as a model for approaching the sometimes contentious issue of women in church leadership roles.

PRAYER

Dear God, you, in your infinite wisdom, have chosen women to be leaders in the church and in the lives of our African peoples. You chose to protect us through those mothers who cradled us across the Middle Passage. You chose Sojourner Truth to guide us to freedom and to state with pride, "And ain't I a woman?" You put honeyed words into the mouths of such gifted poets as Maya Angelou, whose meter calls you blessed. Creative economic genius was laid at the feet of Oprah Winfrey. Prophetic words are spoken by scores of women in ministry whose names have been changed by you. Unnamed sisters have for generations done excellent work in the back rooms of our churches. Finally, dear Lord, your Son, our Christ, was born of a woman, Mary. The honor of female birth is one that you have allowed us to share with Jesus. For this rich celestial and earthly inheritance, we thank you. Amen.

PREACHING

The saints say that you have not preached until you declare the Resurrection. Those who declared the resurrection of Christ were women, namely, Mary Magdalene, Joanna, and Mary the mother of James (see Luke 24:10). Preach a series about strong women in the Bible, beginning with a focus on African women such as Hagar (see Genesis 16; 21:8-21), Zipporah (see Exodus 2:21-22; 4:24-26; Numbers 12:1), the Queen of Sheba (see 1 Kings 10:1-13; 2 Chronicles 9:1-9), and Candace, Queen of the Ethiopians (see Acts 8:27). Pastors can also present modern nonbiblical "she-roes" of African descent as models that women in our churches can emulate. Pastors can utilize the *African American Heritage Hymnal* to find litanies, songs, and other resources that focus on how women have contributed to strengthening the church.

PARISHIONER AWARENESS

Share stories about what women have done for the church. Though not an African American, Anne Marbury Hutchinson provides an instructive story. Mrs. Hutchinson, who lived from 1595 to 1643, is responsible, in important ways, for the founding of Harvard College. Acknowledged as "the mother of New England's first and most serious theological schism"[9] (known as the Antinomian Controversy), she was accused of heresy and sedition for her outspoken views on religion and for providing user-friendly theology classes for women. Her crime, for which she was found guilty in a civil trial in 1638 and banished from the Massachusetts State Colony, was to best noted male preachers, theologians, magistrates, and religious scholars at their arguments, despite the fact that, since she was a woman, she was not formally trained in theology. Her classes had been tolerated only when she focused on scriptural interpretation. Her heresy was to criticize the church, a privilege of magistrates and the clergy, though one rarely used even by them.

Feeling constrained by the guidelines of the Anglican Church, this minister's daughter believed in the soul's liberty. She claimed for herself the "authority of the Spirit and an inner light." At her trial, in response to the charge that she had traduced the laws of church and state, she replied, "As I understand it, laws, commands, rules and edicts are for those who have not the light which makes plain the pathway."[10] Harvard College was started, in part, to provide an excellent education for a new generation of ministers, theologians, and other learned men, training that would allow them never again to lose an argument to a woman such as Mrs. Hutchinson, and to protect society against any such other gender-relevant aberrations, particularly in the realm of faith.

PERSPECTIVE(S) ON PROBLEMS

The Scripture that is most often interpreted to indicate that women are not called into ministry is 1 Timothy 3, which states that overseers are to be men as it discusses the gender of their mates and their responsibilities within that relationship and their stature in the outside community:

> Now the overseer must be above reproach, the husband of but one wife, temperate, self-controlled, respectable, hospitable, able to teach, not given to drunkenness, not violent but gentle, not quarrelsome, not a lover of money. He must manage his own family well and see that his children obey him with proper respect. (If anyone does not know how to manage his own family, how can he take care of God's church?) He must not be a recent convert, or he may become conceited and fall under the same judgment as the devil. He must also have a good reputation with outsiders, so that he will not fall into disgrace and into the devil's trap. (1 Timothy 3:2-7, NIV)

Deacons are discussed in much the same way in verses 8 through 10:

> Deacons, likewise, are to be men worthy of respect, sincere, not indulging in much wine, and not pursuing dishonest gain. They must keep hold of the deep truths of the faith with a clear conscience. They must first be tested; and then if there is nothing against them, let them serve as deacons. (1 Timothy 3:8-10, NIV)

While these verses are very specific in their discussion of the need for priests and deacons to be male for the good of women, families, and the greater society, it is important to remember that the Bible was written in a social time far different from our own.[11] In contrast, the prophet Joel found that service to God was a gender-neutral calling:

> "I will pour out my Spirit on all people.
> Your sons and daughters will prophesy,
> your old men will dream dreams,
> your young men will see visions." (Joel 2:28, NIV)

Note the following text as well:

> I commend to you our sister Phoebe, a servant of the church in Cenchrea. I ask you to receive her in the Lord in a way worthy of the saints and to give her any help she may need from you, for she has been a great help to many people, including me. (Romans 16:1-2, NIV)

Henry Beecher Hicks Jr. writes:

> The authorities are clear that the word *diakonos* which is used of servants in the male sense, is the same word that is used to describe Phoebe. Some, indeed, suggest that deaconesses were really not made in the early church. There are three reasons, however, which I suggest for the establishment of female deacons. (1) ...to deny the

service of any individual, either male or female, is to challenge or denigrate God's intentional value of his creative product. It is only in light of progressive revelation—the more we study God, the more we know about Him—that we understand that God created man and woman in His image; there the works of humankind are not limited by gender or sex. (2) I believe that the word *diakonos* is never used to describe a person, rather it is used to describe a function. Deacon is not a noun which describes a person, but rather a verb which describes one's actions. Ultimately, God uses whom He chooses, whether to teach or to preach, or to serve as deacon within the administrative boundaries of the local congregation. (3) Because Paul is used most often to substantiate the requirement that deacons must be men, it is reasonable to turn to Paul to understand why the reverse must also be the case. Paul speaks, in the book of Galatians, of those who challenge his authority as a preacher of the Gospel and who have infiltrated the church at Galatia with all manner of spurious teaching. Specifically, there are those who want to be Christians while at the same time adhering strictly to the old Judaic law (Judiazers). Paul then makes this argument to those who are bound by tradition and the law.[12]

With respect to attitude, women who wish to gain access to leadership in the church must do it in ways that do not threaten men who may feel as if they are losing powerful roles. Women who find such upfront leadership uncomfortable may want to prayerfully ask themselves how God wants them to use their competence and gifts. Men who are concerned about the encroachment of women may need to think about what gift of God is missing if women are excluded. Men who support women may need to put on suits of armor and bravely support them, even when their role is not met with popularity.

PRACTICAL SOLUTIONS
Churches may want to consider making a rule that language that denigrates women is not allowed. Especially with our youth, this will

create conflicts in some cases about how language is used, often without thinking, as well as about the kind of music (especially female-bashing forms) that is embraced.

Provide an alternative Bible in the pews that focuses on the perspectives of women. *The Women of Color Study Bible* (see Appendix E) is an excellent resource for this purpose. Teach classes on women in the Bible, with a particular focus on women of African descent.

PROGRAMS AND PREMISES

Proactive approaches to problem solving are essential. If, in this case, a group of women feel that they are not being heard by men in the church, it may be smarter to recall the old childhood adage that it is better to be seen than heard. Doing good by doing well in program development (aided by the additional negotiation steps recommended, as well as the expectation and experience of working with supportive men of God) can be a step toward proactive leadership.[13]

Make a difference. Our sisters in Africa have many needs that can be addressed through missions projects. Consider whether your church wants to work with women with HIV/AIDS or those who are being forced into sexual slavery, or develop a unique project. Many denominations have programs that are now working in Africa.

Organize women's programs for excellence. Be certain that the woman's domain is in superb order. It is difficult to ask for equity when one's house has demonstrable flaws.

Mentor young girls and women. Through Christian organizations, denominational groups, the YWCA, the Boys and Girls Club, or other local groups, conduct a regular mentoring project that has as its end goal high school graduation and college attendance.

Be a good neighbor. The women's ministry might consider the adoption of a local female-headed family or an organization that serves women and children (such as a women's shelter). Through the leadership of the women's ministry, the church can become actively involved in assisting the family or organization and bring Christ's love and peace to someone in need.

PASTORAL MANAGEMENT

For female and male pastors, after you pray, consider the following if gender discussions become challenging:

Are my frustrations real?

Do they matter in light of the big picture of my ministry?

Who or what causes them?

How can I minimize my smoldering stress points?

Do my frustrations flourish in some climates I create?[14]

PROMISES

"A woman in harmony with her spirit is like a river flowing."[15] Our churches need to assure that women, who have historically contributed to church growth and wish to contribute to the church's future, are provided with increased opportunities to be in meaningful leadership.

taking off the shackles

What might your church be able to do to raise the status of women?

Would your church be uncomfortable with female leaders? Why or why not?

Given the different social, political, and economic context under which women now exist, should 1 Timothy 3 be understood in a different light to accept women into church leadership roles?

Not all women think that women are ready for leadership in the church. What concerns might women have about the readiness of their sisters and themselves to lead?

How can women express in sensitive, nonthreatening, and conflict-easing ways their desire to serve as leaders?

7

homosexuality

"So when you are offering your gift at the altar, if you remember
that your brother or sister has something against you, leave your
gift there before the altar and go; first be reconciled to your
brother or sister, and then come and offer your gift."

—Matthew 5:23-24, NRSV

I T IS DIFFICULT TO FIND AN ISSUE IN THE CHURCH THAT IS MORE DIVI-
sive than the issue of homosexuality. For many years, it has been
a topic of conversation, study, and intense emotional debate in
mainline denominational churches. Indeed it threatens to divide them.
It is an issue that, to a large extent, is considered taboo in African
American denominations and churches.

Many in the church at large routinely disagree on issues of foreign
policy or taxation. They also take sides on theological questions related to modes of baptism or the eternal status of nonbelievers. In
most of these areas, people, regardless of where they stand, are able to
worship comfortably next to one another. They are able to "agree to
disagree" and then move on, focusing on what they have in common
instead of what divides them.

Such is not usually the case with the issue of homosexuality. For
some with conservative views, there is no room for discussion.
Typically, they view homosexuality as an indication of where people
stand on the authority of Scripture. They maintain that the Bible is
clear that homosexual behavior is sinful. Some with more liberal perspectives—who maintain that Bible passages cited to oppose homosexuality have been taken out of context—are equally set in their
views. Some routinely dismiss their opponents' positions, no matter

how carefully researched or sincerely held, as attributable to "homo-phobia," defined as the irrational fear of homosexuals.

Indeed, the temptation exists in a book of this nature to simply avoid the topic so as not to risk offending people on one side of the debate or the other. But to ignore the topic would be to violate one of the essential principles for addressing conflict: We cannot manage conflict if we run from it or pretend that it does not exist.

While some African American congregations accept homosexual persons fully, the majority hold to the traditional view that the Bible opposes homosexual behavior. This view stands in tension with the natural tendency of African American Christians, in light of their history in this country, to be loving and accepting toward others, in spite of whatever personal history or struggles they might bring to God's house. People in the church realize that homosexual persons are among their neighbors, family members, pastors, and church members. As a result of the ambivalence toward the issue of homosexuality, many congregations tend to avoid the topic, thus by default adopting a sort of informal "don't ask, don't tell" policy. This approach has sometimes made it difficult for churches, regardless of their position on homosexuality, to address the HIV/AIDS epidemic (exacerbated by men who are on the "down low") that has challenged the health resources of our community.

the 8 p's

It is not the purpose of this book to determine who is right and who is wrong. Rather, the goal is to provide information and perspectives to help manage the conflict in this area, conflict that will not go away any time soon. Even in the midst of our differences, it is important for people in the church to find common ground where possible and to express their disagreements—thereby listening to and learning from one another—with compassion and understanding. As with other areas of conflict, it is my hope that the 8 P's model can contribute to this goal.

PRAYER

When we disagree intensely with others on an issue that is important to us, it is sometimes difficult to view them as people who have feelings, struggles, and good reasons for believing what they believe. It is important to pray for those others. The Bible tells us to pray for our enemies. While people who believe in Jesus Christ and his teachings ought never consider one another enemies, there is a sense in which those on opposite sides of this conflict are at war. The beautiful *Evening Prayer*, a song that my paternal grandmother, Virginia Ruth Berry McKinney, used to sing to me, can help each side deal with their struggles and embattled hearts.

> If I have wounded any soul today,
> If I have caused one foot to go astray,
> If I have walked in my own willful way,
> Dear Lord, forgive!
> If I have uttered idle words or vain,
> If I have turned aside from want or pain,
> Lest I myself shall suffer through the strain,
> Dear Lord, forgive!
> If I have been perverse or hard, or cold,
> If I have longed for shelter in Thy fold,
> When Thou hast given me some fort to hold,
> Dear Lord, forgive!
> Forgive the sins I have confessed to Thee;
> Forgive the secret sins I do not see;
> O guide me, love me and my keeper be,
> Dear Lord, Amen.[1]

PREACHING

Many a preacher has surely struggled with regard to what to say from the pulpit when it comes to difficult and divisive issues such as homosexuality. This is particularly the case when the congregation is divided. The preacher, of course, must be true to his or her own convictions. Yet there are messages preachers can communicate that cut across the antipathy opponents feel for one another. All preachers, for example, ought to be able to proclaim that, regardless of a person's sexual orientation, he or she is still a person, created in God's image, in need of God's love, and deserving of protection from those in our society who would harm them. All preachers can espouse the message that we see through a glass darkly, and that it is important not only to understand but also to respect the sincere motives of those with whom we disagree. Preaching moments are teaching moments. However, this teaching need not always consist of taking definitive, opposite, or oppositional stands. It can also address the attitudes and processes by which we form our positions and by which we live and worship among those with whom we disagree.

PARISHIONER AWARENESS
Many people on both sides of the debate have formed positions without being as knowledgeable as they should be with regard to various biblical, theological, sociological, and psychological considerations. Perhaps no amount of awareness will change a person's mind one way or the other on the issue itself, but it could change perspectives on how to understand and treat those with differing perspectives.

Churches and individuals should be challenged to move beyond citing only those researchers or theologians who uphold their viewpoint. In addition to any new knowledge that is actually acquired, the very experience of trying to gain greater understanding can defuse anger, confusion, and fear.

PERSPECTIVE(S) ON PROBLEMS
Because of the complexity of this debate, it behooves us all to enter it humbly. Regardless of where we stand on homosexuality, we should all be able to affirm that the church is for everyone. It is the perfect place for sinners of all kinds, for those in need of God's grace, love, and help.

Those with conservative views need to be wary of the presupposition that tradition is always good. Long-held traditions of the church have sometimes proved to be misguided and unbiblical. On the other hand, those with liberal views ought not presuppose that new is always authoritative. Traditional views should be fully understood and respected before being dismissed.

Many on both sides of the debate will be tempted to become angry and judgmental. Keep in mind the goal that others will see God in you. Whether pastor or parishioner, God's love must be visible in our hearts, our voices, our embraces, and our eyes. Again, we must try to understand the positions of others, even if we do not agree with them. Such understanding is communicated not only by our words, but also by our behavior. And no discussion of this kind is genuine unless people enter into it with open minds, with a willingness to be open to one another and to perspectives that create the potential for God to work in our lives.

PRACTICAL SOLUTIONS
Some churches might choose to hold open discussions or forums around homosexuality. In these settings, it is very important for people to feel that their voices, though diverse, are being heard and that whatever fears and concerns they have will be addressed. Because the topic is so volatile, it is advisable for churches that want to hold open conversations to make use of professional facilitators not affiliated with a specific position relative to the homosexuality debate.

PROGRAMS AND PREMISES
Rather than having people wonder what the church believes, it makes sense for churches to adopt policies on homosexuality consistent with their theological positions and values. As outlined above, regardless of a church's position, churches ought to encourage open and loving discussion. And they should look for opportunities, including through the development or implementation of caring

ministries, to reach out in love to homosexual persons regardless of the church's theological stance.

One ministry possibility is to arrange and conduct a special prayer service during worship or some other time in the week in which the doors of the church are opened to anyone who feels in need of God's love. Pray that people will feel loved by God and will take steps to draw closer to God. The Bible says, "Whoever is thirsty, let him come; and whoever wishes, let him take the free gift of the water of life" (Revelation 22:17, NIV).

Churches also have the opportunity for ministry among victims of AIDS, which of course is not an exclusively "gay disease," though it began within and continues to have high rates in the homosexual community. African Americans comprise 12.3 percent of the total population in the United States, yet account for more than half (54%) of the 42,000 new HIV infections each year. African Americans also have the worst survival rates of all ethnic groups. The AIDS diagnosis rate is 23 percent higher among African American women than it is among white women and nine times higher among African American men than white men. To reach out in compassion to those who are suffering is to follow in Christ's footsteps. And such actions can serve to unify believers even in the midst of disagreements.

PASTORAL MANAGEMENT

If policies regarding homosexuality have become an area of significant conflict in the church, then a conflict assessment is an essential step in conflict management and resolution. An assessment will assist the pastor in understanding the concerns of all parties. Conflict assessment is a learning process for the church that builds relationships, develops a shared knowledge base, offers insights into the type of intervention that is most likely to work, and provides input into designing a work plan for an intervention that is likely to be reasonably successful.[2] Conflict Assessment consists of the following:[3]

Introduction. Together with church leadership and an outside resource (from a conflict management organization or the local college or university), the pastor should determine the different perspectives represented in the conflict (stakeholders) and, from that, develop a clear mandate (goal).

Information gathering. Using strategic open-ended questions, data is gathered by the neutral facilitator in stakeholder interviews in the form of a survey or focus groups. The results of the interviews and surveys should allow an understanding of how the conflict developed, key issues related to the conflict, basic interests of the involved factions, barriers to discussion, and important issues for future discussion.

Analysis. Findings are summarized, with the summary including the mapping of areas of agreement and disagreement. The analysis should be integrative in nature, meaning that it should emphasize common interests, positions, and goals so that consensus can be built. Information should be shared with church leadership.

Process design. Goals, agendas, and group representatives should be selected to participate in working on the issue, with a definitive timeline. Note that two sides with different viewpoints must work together toward consensus.

Report writing, feedback, distribution. Findings, in concise written form, should be presented to the church membership in an open and facilitated meeting for feedback and discussion.

This method of conflict assessment can be applied to all areas that create conflict in the African American church. The membership takes its cues from the pastor. If pastors can be true leaders and can use available pastoral management tools (from preaching to assessment) as required, the pew will follow in kind.

PROMISES

The promise of the African American church lies in its taking a more proactive approach to homosexuality regardless of where it might lead. Christ provides an excellent model. He did not ostracize community members; rather, he embraced those on the fringes of society, understanding that they, more than anyone, needed love and acceptance. Such acceptance comes from the heart and has little to do with theological constraints. As was said at the beginning of the chapter, conflict that is left unaddressed cannot be resolved.

taking off the shackles

What is your assessment of what the Bible has to say about homosexuality?

What is your assessment of what the Bible says about how homosexual persons should be treated?

What is your assessment about why African Americans appear to have tendencies toward "homophobia"?

If persons of homosexual orientation were to attend your church for a month, would they feel comfortable?

What could be done in your church setting to address conflicts surrounding homosexuality?

If your church is divided on this issue, what are some principles or commitments that could lead to greater unity?

8

church migration

"I am the gate; whoever enters through me will be saved."
(John 10:9, NIV)

FOR AFRICAN AMERICAN CHRISTIANS, THE CHURCH PROVIDES A bridge—across history, across troubled waters, and into a God-promised future. For many, our place of greatest solace and comfort outside of our own homes—in many cases, even more than our own homes—is our church home. It is where many of the most important moments of our lives have occurred, and it is the place where we spend hours each week in worship as well as involved in service to others. We often have family history in a particular church. Churches are the places where our grandmothers sang in the choir, our mothers served on missions committees, or our fathers were ushers. Those who move to another city typically seek out a church that reminds them of their home church. Perhaps it is something familiar and comfortable about the preacher or the choir or the style of the building that draws us to the new "church home."

What is fascinating about our connection to our churches is that we are attached, as is the case with our homes, to the physical sites. We want certain architectural features to be a part of our churches; we have expectations regarding how a church should look. It is a place with a spire, perhaps, or beautiful stained glass. For many, the church must have wooden pews with compartments for Bibles, hymnals, and communion glasses. Yet others seek communal halls from which waft the familiar scent of true church chicken!

But is this truly what a church *has* to be? I once served on a committee that was looking at church buildings that might serve as models for a potential move. One building we looked at was built in new, megachurch architectural form, with stadium seating, no interior windows, and plasma television screens mounted behind the pulpit on which the service was presented in Internet format (not the TV-screen video feed now common in many churches). I was aware that God was in the building, but it did not *feel* like church to me. I realized, however, that I had grown up in traditional and historic church buildings, and that this building was designed with people quite unlike me in mind. This church, ministering to an MTV-generation of relatively new Christians with shorter attention spans than I, and attuned to quick-cut television formats, had appropriately focused on bringing Christ to a generation of people with a different learning modality. I was quite impressed that the church had structured itself for its specific community, though it was clear I was not part of that community.

And therein, as Hamlet says, lies the (conflicting) rub. Churches are changing and growing in many ways—demographically, architecturally, and in their locations—to adjust to the needs and wants of their parishioners and of the people they are trying to reach. As a result, there is great potential for conflict around any of several different issues. One is the choice of churches to leave urban areas and, in doing so, potentially remove essential faith and social service resources from the city, thus leaving African Americans in surrounding, often historic, community without easy access to the many faith and social services that our churches tend to provide.

Another issue is the change in the style of the church services to adapt to the shifting demographic. Some churches, as noted above, are built around the needs of their specific demographic population. Sometimes young pastors attempt to introduce styles that might not mesh with the diverse needs of the church demographic. (While this chapter will not address this issue, the concern most often noted is that the richness of Afri-Christian musical traditions is being lost.[1])

Questions related to moves to suburban areas certainly apply to megachurches. In fact, conflict has arisen in relation to the increasing number of megachurches in the African American community.

(Megachurches are those congregations in excess of 2,000 members. Some have memberships as large as 30,000.) Large urban churches often move to the suburbs where they can adequately grow to accommodate their congregations and ministries. Such churches may not offer the familial worship environment that facilitates the warmth of smaller churches or that provides easy opportunities for some interpersonal needs to be discerned and met. And though no research exists to support this supposition, pastors report that in any move, parishioners are lost. Often parishioners who live in the city will not drive to the suburbs to attend church. Parishioners who feel that the church, by leaving the urban center, has abandoned its history or the needs of the neighborhood, are unlikely to move with it, regardless of their earlier commitment to the church.

The fact that what are typically described as megachurches are usually nondenominational and typically founded by highly visible charismatic leaders who often preach a gospel of prosperity is also a source of conflict, especially in cases where the church is managed in a nepotistic manner that does not easily allow for congregational scrutiny and organizational and fiscal transparency.[2]

thinking it through

Making a decision to move God's house ought never to be done cavalierly. Following are some of the questions that should be asked: Does a move outside an urban center reflect a move away from the traditional congregational base? Does it mean that the church is leaving people in the city who need services and ministries best provided by the church? Should the church explore new architectural styles that are focused on the desires of twenty-first-century Christians? Or should it honor history through the use of more traditional church architecture? Does the African American church do a disservice to the mission of Christ by moving to the suburbs? Does it necessarily do a disservice to the community by leaving? Does it, by increasing when it can to megachurch size, lose the ties that bind us together as an effective community? Or does it simply replace them with a new model of ministry?

Certainly there are instances of moving from urban centers to suburban locations (or, in some cases, making what are perceived as unnecessary architectural changes to historic urban churches)[3] that are the brainchild of those who wish to impose their egos on the landscape of the temple. Thus, in the process of determining reasons for why a move is essential, pastors must be prayerful that ego does not cause history to be destroyed and that humility is among the characteristics with which God graces them. Congregations, too, must consider this move as carefully as they would their family home, understanding it to be the home in which their church and community family will do the Lord's work.

the 8 p's

The Rev. Wendell Griffen of Little Rock, Arkansas, a minister and judge, states that "in its best form, the black church is characterized by three essential traits: (1) redemptive fellowship, (2) active and intentional ministry focused on social, political, and economic, as well as personal and corporate liberation from satanic oppression, and (3) prophetic efforts to proclaim and personify the grace and truth of God in our time and place."[4] When viewed in this manner, it becomes clear that our *place* can, in fact, be essential to our mission. Where we do our work can be important. It is why, after all, we engage in international missions, going into all the world. While we consider our local evangelical efforts to be essential to our work for Christ, we are not always as intentional about the placement of our temples. We hear stories of churches that, for lack of good financial planning, lose their churches or of churches that have received parcels of land as political favors.

Our evangelical efforts, the growth of our churches, and our effective management efforts will lead many churches to rebuild in the city and in suburban areas. In all building efforts, pastor and people should maintain open communication about the purpose of the venture, as well as about the historic and future purpose of the black church, so that wherever we are the Word can become flesh and live among us, full of grace and truth (see John 1:14).

Let's use the 8 P's model now to further delve into the process of getting to Amen.

PRAYER

Church moves require the faith of all involved—pastor, lay leaders, and congregation. Alternate lyrics of the song "The Church's One Foundation" serve as prayer for the questions that have been raised about whether moving away from a urban center is the correct decision and, if that decision has been made, how to do it in a way that honors congregation and community, even when that congregation grows large.

> The Church's one foundation is Christ, God's own true Child
> In whom the whole creation is freed and reconciled
> To bring the Church together, Christ lived and freely died;
> Raised up by God, forever, Christ lives to be our Guide.[5]

Regardless of the final locations of our congregations, if we remember that our foundation is to be centered on Christ and model our personal and institutional behavior on Christ, then we will be more likely to find conflict-neutral ways to "bring our churches together" in a manner that is "freed and reconciled."

PREACHING

Christians, because we are human, are a decidedly fractious lot. Deacons fight over policy and positions, sisters threaten to tear out each other's weaves or stomp on each other's hats (and sometimes do), and preachers fight from the pulpit in ways that cause rancor in the pews. And the gossip we hear, whether true or not, is painful, prurient, and unkind. The pain of a potential church move, particularly if the move is away from a historic church, creates many potential fights, problems with church policies, and the burning up of phone lines on Sunday evening. The knowledge that these are the anticipated outcomes to any move provides pastors with opportunities to preach parishioners past their significant concerns about losing their church home.

PARISHIONER AWARENESS

Information regarding a potential move should get from the church leadership to the congregation as quickly as possible. To decrease the potential for conflict in this area (and it is great), transparency is the best policy.

Church leaders ought to communicate openly at each step of the way. Finances (since a portion of fund-raising efforts include church members), architectural plans, and reports on possible church styles gleaned from visits to other church buildings, must be shared with parishioners. Church walls have ears, and the gossip likely to surface if plans for a church move are made without full disclosure will be worse than if the truth is shared. If church leaders have a vision about why the church must move, there will be excitement in the pews about the growth of God's house and cooperation with plans for that growth.

Church moves can be traumatic. After all, we are talking about the place where people found the Lord, got married, buried loved ones, experienced moving sermons weekly, and have had myriad meaningful experiences. Because it is their home—and that is how it is referred to (our church home)—people in the pew need to be an active part of any decision to move the church to another location. That can occur in the following ways:

■ An assessment process in which a neutral outside agency assists the church in determining the need for a move to another location. Reasonable examples necessitating a move include: overcrowding with minimal local options for growth, prohibitive urban land construction costs, conflicts between the local neighborhood and the church, and a proportion of parishioners already living in the location identified for the potential church move.

■ Focus groups in which neutral outside facilitators learn from parishioners their viewpoints on a potential move.

■ A survey that assesses viewpoints of all church members. Unlike focus groups, the survey is an instrument that parishioners answer in private.

■ A vote that definitively demonstrates the perspective of all church members (defined denominationally as tithing members or as adults over the age of eighteen) on the preliminary decision and the final church move. Baptists must, as a congregational body, vote for such a move. This may, however, be a good idea for other denominational groups as well, even if the decision cannot be binding in the same way. The vote can, at a minimum, determine the will of the congregation, which is important information and will help the congregation feel, if the other options are also used, that their voices have been heard.

PERSPECTIVE(S) ON PROBLEMS

The Art of Possibility is a book of leadership skills shared by an unusual husband and wife team. Rosamund Stone Zander is a family therapist and landscape painter. Her husband, Benjamin Zander, is the conductor of the Boston Philharmonic Orchestra. Based on their experiences as life partners and artists who understand the melding of their craft with the organizational systems inherent in their professions, they offer a set of practices to assist leaders. Their practices are based on the simple premises that life is composed as a story and that we are capable of much more than we tend to believe. As nontraditional conflict management strategies, these practices are useful ways of looking at groups from positions of strength. This practice, "Leading from Any Chair," describes the manner in which a conductor grants greatness to all of his or her musicians.

> The conductor decides who is playing in his orchestra. Even when he comes in fresh to guest-conduct players who are already in their seats, he determines who is there. When he sees instrumentalists who look listless, he can decide that they are bored and resigned, or he can greet in them the original spark that

enticed them into music, now dimmed to a flicker. He can say, "Of course! They have had to go against their passionate natures and interrupt the long line of their commitment on account of the many competing demands in the music professions. They want to be recognized as the true artists they really are." He can see, sitting before him, the jaded and the disaffected—or the tender and the glorious lover of music.

A monumental question for leaders in any organization to consider is: How much greatness are we willing to grant people? Because it makes all the difference at every level who it is we decide we are leading. The activity of leadership is not limited to conductors, presidents, and CEOs of course—the player who energizes the orchestra by communicating his newfound appreciation for the tasks of the conductor, or a parent who fashions in her own mind that her children desire to contribute (or the church trustee, or the new member who volunteers to head the food drive for homeless women and children), is exercising leadership of the most profound kind."[6]

Moving the church home requires coordinated orchestration from the pulpit to the pew, one that requires among church leadership the capacity to define "church" holistically and to open up the opportunity for leadership from any chair.

PRACTICAL SOLUTIONS
Churches often assume that the existence of weekly prayer meetings and an array of classes will facilitate relationships. Because research demonstrates that prayer groups and Bible study ease depression and loneliness that may result from a church move, it is essential that programs be monitored, assigning prayer partners, inviting cell groups to meet for quarterly dinners, having youth pizza parties with the pastor, and sponsoring new member Question-and-Answer sessions with the pastor. These are but a few small group activities that can serve to create a sense of family in churches as they move.

Mark Buchanan shares four spiritual disciplines to keep conflict from scarring our souls. Transformed from war into an orientation for healing ourselves, Buchanan believes we have:

■ *A spirit of heartbreak.* Bitterness, rage, anger, slander, and all incivility toward one another grieves the Holy Spirit. It should break our hearts as well. "To be a minister of reconciliation begins when we grieve with the One who grieves."[7]

■ *A spirit of giddiness.* Find, even in tense moments of conflict, joy in the Lord. "Conflict within the church almost always stems from a failure to live by faith and not by sight. Taking our eyes off Jesus easily entangles us in sin and distraction and quickly we lose heart. Thus, rejoicing in the Lord is reality therapy."[8]

■ *A spirit of hardness.* Conflict causes us, oftentimes, to make our hearts hard. Instead, says Buchanan, we need to learn to keep our hearts warm toward each other but set our "faces like flint," and pray together with Psalm 127.

■ *A spirit of humility.* As difficult as it is to do, we must remind ourselves of our own shortcomings when we enter a conflict. We live among and are ourselves people with unclean lips. If we enter any situation asking the Lord to refine us, we stand a much better chance of working through our conflict. Buchanan suggests praying David's prayer, Psalm 139:23-24.[9]

PROGRAMS AND PREMISES

Following the Holocaust, the Jewish diasporic community determined that they would never forget what had happened to them. From ceremonial components of a unified faith, to the support of religious and secular Jews for the state of Israel (if not all of its policies), to the maintenance of oral history of the Holocaust through projects such as the Shoah Visual History Foundation, the Jewish community finds a number of ways to remember important and painful parts of their history. While it may not seem that the move of an individual African American church from an urban center to the suburbs takes on the import of the remembrance faith traditions of the Jewish people, in each move is the possibility that history is lost. As Joel Kotkin, the author of *Tribes*, demonstrated, through the omission in his book of the African peoples as a group who would be strategic to the world's future beyond the twentieth century (see chapter 1), slavery has deliberately separated us from our memories.

Through our churches, we have worked to create what educational systems have frequently not found important enough to provide for us, or have, in many cases, inaccurately taught us. The conflict, then, of moving the urban church out of urban centers too quickly can be the moving of essential history. Stories are told of pastors who, primarily for reasons of ego, wish to tear down historic temples of God and rebuild them in the suburbs, when there are opportunities through negotiations with city agencies to rebuild in the city on parcels of land equal to what would be gained in the suburbs and at nearly comparable prices. There are very legitimate reasons for churches to move locations, obviously, but essential questions, as noted in "Thinking it Through" (p. 81–82) and in the "Taking Off the Shackles" section at the end of this chapter, should always be asked about what is gained and lost for the community with such a move. It should always be the goal of any move to preserve and maintain church history, lest we forget, not just Gethsemane, but our church, ethnic, and spiritual histories.

Church conflict related to moving can be reduced though the maintenance of history. This history can be embraced through the use of Africentric architecture in the building of the new temple; utilization of local diasporic architects and artisans; development of the church archive in paper, DVD, and web formats that include church history and the stories of church elders (see the model provided by the National Visionary Leadership Project[10] and the Survivors of the Shoah Visual History Foundation[11]); and incorporation through art of local community Afri-Christian history. For example, each city has stories to tell. These local stories—in mural, poem, or story form, essential to the life of the original church—can become part of the new church and, by their presence, create a link of historical continuity between the urban and suburban sites.

PASTORAL MANAGEMENT

In his book describing the challenge of moving a church from the inner city to the suburbs, the Rev. Dr. H. Beecher Hicks Jr. writes about the problem Moses had in getting the people of Israel to share the authenticity of his vision for building a tabernacle (Exodus 25:1-9). Stating the importance of having a defined strategy and gaining consensus for any move or new building process, Dr. Hicks states:

> There seem to be at least two things wrong with the vision Moses said God gave to him. First, Moses had a vision but no strategy. I don't know much about modern management theory, but I do know that if you have a vision without a strategy, all you really have is an illusion. A vision without a strategy isn't going anywhere. Merely speaking a vision isn't enough. At some point, somebody is going to want to know how you're going to make the vision become reality. Vision provides directions, but a strategy is needed to determine how that vision will be carried to completion.
>
> Moses' vision was flawed in a second way: He had no process for building consensus. Consensus building is a process by which collective agreement is obtained. Through consensus building, an idea garners support with the hope of gaining approval. It is difficult to achieve a vision unless everyone is given the opportunity to give input on the goals, objectives, and values the vision endorses. Consensus building is necessary to achieve the "buy-in" that is needed before a vision can become viable....[12]

A church move demands much of the pastor in terms of leadership and management skills. Church members want to hear the plans regarding the move through specially called meetings, in sermons, in ministry meetings, and in other, creative ways that are part of the decision-making process. The pastor must come to the congregation with all documents in order, ready to answer any questions and understanding that some church members will be angry with the move no matter what. Some people don't mind leaving an old house, while other people will hang on to the pillars while the movers are loading up the truck! It is the pastor's job to set the vision, acknowledge the fears, take nothing for granted, and most important, keep no secrets from the congregation.

PROMISES

The noun *promise* is defined as "the assurance that something will be done" or "will turn out well." Building Christ's temple requires a vast array of promises that lead to the completion of a structure that then houses a place where promises to Christ can, in fact, be kept. Christ, of course, does not require a temple to keep his promises to us. For us, the task of building is an exercise in discipline, in organization, in fiscal short- and long-term planning, and in strategic planning. It is also a challenge to our capacity to get past the conflicts that arise regarding the emotional and functional aspects of moving, enhancing our properties if our decision is to stay put, or simply of having the conversation.

According to Peacemaker Ministries,

> When a local church teaches its people to live out the gospel in the conflicts of daily life, people are more willing to admit their shortcomings and ask for help before a crisis occurs. Families are better equipped to handle disputes, which makes divorce less likely. Members are encouraged to go to each other to discuss problems instead of letting them fester. The church is protected from division and splits, and offended members are less likely to leave. As a result, church growth is improved.[13]

Whatever and wherever the venue of our new church, the promise of a new temple is the opportunity to enhance the work that we do for Christ, and the manner in which we do it structures the promise. A temple filled with bad tempers may find it difficult to meet Christ at the door.

taking off the shackles

If we are planning to move our church from the city to the suburbs, how can the church best honor all aspects of our history (church history—pastoral, time line of important events, "saints" important to the life of the church, ministry presidents, etc.—and local community history)?

Is the community voice being heard in any decision to move?

If the church has determined to move because of low attendance, have neighbors been surveyed to determine why they are not attending?

What services might be essential to the needs of the community? What plans can be made to maintain "services in the city" after a suburban move?

How can pastors protect against hubris of building monuments to themselves rather than to Christ?

What are the best ways to honor church history through architecture while addressing the technological needs of the twenty-first-century church and meeting the broad range of parishioners' needs to whom ministry must occur?

What strategies, from surveys to focus groups, are planned to communicate effectively with the pew about any potential church move?

If, through an assessment process, the church learns that a move is not in the best interest of the church, how can that information be effectively managed among the different church factions?

9
politics and preaching

"America has two great dominant strands of
political thought; we're represented up here on
this stage: conservatism, which at its very best draws
lines that should not be crossed; and progressivism,
which at its very best breaks down barriers that
are no longer needed or should never have
been erected in the first place."[1]

THE AME CHURCH BEGAN, IN PART, WITH A GOAL OF TEACHING slaves to read. Baptist churches determined to be autonomous so that they could chart their own paths following the too-close "oversight" of slavery. None would deny that the African American church has been, from its inception, a political institution. As it has grown and strengthened, there have, however, been quarters that have been conflicted about its political nature. Preachers with conservative or fundamentalist beliefs have sometimes interpreted the Bible to teach against political involvement. Due in part to a conflict over whether or not to support Martin Luther King Jr.'s political actions, the National Baptist Convention (NBC) split in 1961, resulting in the founding of the Progressive National Baptist Convention (PNBC). This split was evidence of how the line between politics and preaching stressed even those who believed in the political power of the pulpit.[2] (Recognizing the need for resolutions of old conflicts, four Baptist conventions—NBC-USA, Inc., NBC of America, PNBC, and the National Missionary Baptist Convention—have been meeting to work past old rifts.)[3]

wandering africans?

"Sometimes," said syndicated columnist Clarence Page, "I feel as though we African Americans have been wandering through the wilderness for 40 years like the ancient children of Israel, searching for a new agenda."[4] The long-gone agenda about which Page lamented included the bonding of shared geography and economic conditions and had, among its significant components, the black community's standing as a united front on strategic social issues such as voting rights, educational equity, and the eradication of Jim Crow laws. The goals, some believed, grew a middle class and left others behind, loosening the community's bonds. According to other observers, a black leadership industry was also born, the dynamic of which had "very little to do with black people....Underlying these stories about black leaders is the idea that black Americans are a people who need to be led, perpetuating the idea that we are less capable of thinking and acting for ourselves than members of other ethnic or racial groups."[5]

With no such clear and consistently stated shared goals in the twenty-first century, the African American community struggles. That these goals are not shared community-wide is not happenstance and may be, in many cases, deliberate. For example, there are some scholars who believe that so strong was Dr. King's impact on American society that, following his assassination, the communication media (print and television) infrastructure assured that no one single African American received as much coverage as did Dr. King. Important national leaders have emerged—the Rev. Jesse Jackson Sr., Kweisi Mfume (NAACP), Colin Powell, and more leaders—though none have, in fact, had the singular galvanizing national or global impact of Dr. King in highlighting options for peace. In local African American communities, topic-specific leadership has tended to come from black churches (often from the large, most well-established churches), civil rights organizations, coalitions directed toward resolution of specific issues, and "community voice(s)," that person or those persons who can be relied upon to make a mighty noise to bring attention to things that need fixing in the community. Because they are not accustomed to media attention, there have also been terrible leadership examples, however, in which ministers and community leaders, seeing television cameras before them, fight for face time, presenting an embarrassing front to a local community and, on occasion, a nation.[6]

Additionally, though the splits in our community may be holdovers from slavery, we have continued to create artificial distinctions among us. For example, African Americans have significant socioeconomic class divisions, allowing among ourselves the perpetuation of the attendant stereotypes. Finally, the nature of leadership in our country has also changed, as has respect for those whom we consider to be our leaders. As a result, celebrations such as Kwanzaa were designed specifically to assist us with the definition of the factors that we *should* value.

Though African Americans had been a solidly Democratic voting block—regardless of geographical region—for over forty years, in the 2004 election, 11 percent of African American voters voted for President George W. Bush (up from 8 percent in 2000), stating support for the moral values he espoused in spite of their concerns about Republican positions on a number of social issues.

Just as the political parties must try to work across the aisle, those in the church whose conflicting political views have made their work for Christ difficult must prayerfully promise to work across the nave. This entails asking such questions as those that follow:

■ Does the argument have a scriptural basis?

■ What were the historical, socioeconomic, and political contexts of the scriptural basis?

■ Does the Scripture's sociopolitical context have meaning in today's world?

■ What would Jesus do?

the 8 p's

The political nature of African American churches saved and protected us. It taught us to read when reading was illegal, hid us in back rooms until we could be taken north to safety, sat us in rooms to engage voter registration efforts, and provided the platforms from which politicians could speak to us. In all of these political efforts, we understood that, while the nature of our revolutionary action was, in and of itself, political in nature, we respected the separation of church and state, as we did not want government intrusion in our churches.

However, as political parties have made direct calls to create alignments with individual pastors and denominations, many Constitutional scholars, religious believers, and others have become concerned about the survival of this "wall of separation," believing that the line between church and state has eroded significantly. Faith-based efforts have become increasingly popular, particularly among conservative, evangelical Christian groups, while many more theologically liberal Christians voice concerns that the funds associated with those efforts, though serving important needs, may overly involve government in church business, and, in effect, erode the church-state wall.

Part of avoiding, deflecting, or solving conflict is asking questions about the ethics of very difficult situations. Politics are off the topic list at dinner parties because the issues frequently seem insoluble. For those who understand that there are ways to get to Amen, even on the most impossible topics, Kenneth Blanchard and Norman Vincent Peale have developed an ethical checklist for helping leaders determine the source of their motivations:

■ Is it legal? Will I be violating either civil law or [church] policy?

■ Is it balanced? Is it fair to all concerned in the short term as well as the long term? Does it promote win-win relationships?

■ How does it make me feel about myself? Will it make me proud? Would I feel good if my position were published in the newspaper? Would I feel good if my family knew about it?

■ Is it material suitable for prayer? Is it something I am pleased to discuss with God? Or do I prefer to keep it with myself?

■ [For pastors] Does it support my ordination vows? Does it reflect the motivations I perceived when I was ordained? If my actions were publicly announced tomorrow, would it reflect well on my colleagues in professional ministry?[7]

Certainly, many African American pastors have typically lived the church-state balance well within its historical bounds, understanding that "the separation of church and state does not mean the separation of values from our public life."[8] Let's take a closer look now at the 8 P's as strategies for managing this political conflict in the church.

PRAYER

Starting with the honest assessment that conflict inherently involves two sides and that the perceptions related to politico-religious viewpoints often take us far away from Christ, we should start with prayer, an agreement to love each other as we work out our church policies related to the particular issue at hand. When I have come to a place in my life where I have a conflict that seems irresolvable, I ask God's intervention, understanding that I may simply need to pray in this manner: *Dear Lord, bring us past our impasse with dignity and, whatever the final outcome of our challenge, grant our spirits peace. Amen.*

PREACHING

As African American preachers have known for generations, preaching is itself a political act. The sanctuary is a sacred place, certainly, but as the church is part and parcel of society, preaching must address what occurs in the lives of church members, making preaching (once it was no longer illegal for African Americans) decidedly political.

Pastors can preach on political themes in the Bible, or they can cite scriptural support to elucidate community, national, or international issues. "The Spirit of the Lord is on me, because he has anointed me to preach good news to the poor. He has sent me to proclaim freedom for the prisoners and recovery of sight for the blind, to release the oppressed" (Luke 4:18, NIV).

Preachers must recognize, however, that preaching on political principles does not always easily or automatically translate into clear positions on specific political issues. Thus, in this area, perhaps more than any, it is important for preachers to remember the need for humility. In *On Jordan's Stormy Banks: Leading Your Congregation through the Wilderness of Change,* the Rev. H. Beecher Hicks Jr. teaches pastors to consider that their viewpoints and God's may differ:

> If I discover that I am having difficulty understanding the purpose and priorities of the church, it may be because I don't see what God sees. It could be that I don't have a God-centered and God-directed view of what God envisions for the church. My task is to abandon my vision and get in line with God's vision. Doing so will allow me to go where God is going rather than trying to get God in line with where I am going.[9]

PARISHIONER AWARENESS

The people, in a democratic process, are believed to have more wisdom than the few. This is why, with the exception of the electoral college that decides the presidential race, the popular vote determines the winner: "Democracy rules." In his fascinating book *The Wisdom of Crowds*, James Surowiecki, a columnist for *The New Yorker*, extends this argument to the social and economic marketplaces:

> Diversity and independence are important because the best collective decisions are the product of disagreement and conflict, not consensus and compromise. An intelligent group, especially when confronted with cognition problems, does not ask its members to modify its positions in order to let the group reach a decision everyone can be happy with. Instead, it figures out how to use mechanisms—like market prices, or intelligent voting systems—to aggregate and produce collective judgments that represent not what any one person thinks but rather, in some sense, what they all think. Paradoxically, the best way for a group to be smart is for each person to think and act as independently as possible.[10]

While this may sound peculiar, it is important for several reasons: (1) Knowing your own mind is the best way to avoid conflict in the first place and to work through conflict if it does occur. (2) In any conflict resolution session, individuals must bring their well-reasoned ideas to the table. (3) All of the ideas that come to the table, representing a diversity of knowledge and perspectives, if treated with respect, will, like market or voting systems, allow the effective sorting of the best ideas to then occur. Conflicting ideas, healthy in this system because they represent diverse thought rather than angry persons or personalities, increase the possibility of exciting options for the growing church.

PERSPECTIVE(S) ON PROBLEMS

Groupthink, first identified following the Bay of Pigs fiasco[11] during President John Kennedy's tenure, occurs when people cannot see "outside the box." Our tendency is to avoid the discussion of politics altogether or fight about it across an irreconcilable chasm, or because we don't want to do either, get stuck in an agree-to-agree process of groupthink, which is also a poor option. Groupthink is dangerous because members often discredit and explain away viewpoints contrary to group thinking, and members have the illusion of invulnerability, take extreme risk, and are overly optimistic. Members have pressure to conform and apply self-censorship within the group, perceive falsely that everyone agrees with the group's decision, ignore ethical consequences of the decisions, and construct negative stereotypes of rivals outside the group. Some members appoint themselves to the role of protecting the group from adverse information that might threaten group complacency. Groupthink does not encourage diversity of thought.

Work to avoid the possibility of political groupthink by encouraging diversity of thought and attending to the following:

■ The group should be made aware of the causes and consequences of groupthink.

■ The leaders should be neutral, consistently encourage an atmosphere of open inquiry, give high priority to airing objections and doubts, and be accepting of criticism.

■ Groups should always consider unpopular alternatives.

■ Sometimes it is useful to divide the group into two separate deliberative bodies as feasibilities are evaluated.

■ Outside experts should be included in vital decision making.

■ Spend a sizable amount of time considering all opposition from rival groups and organizations.

■ After reaching a preliminary consensus on a decision, all residual doubt should be expressed and the matter reconsidered.

■ Tentative decisions should be discussed with trusted colleagues not in the decision-making group.

■ The organization should follow the administrative practice of establishing several independent decision-making groups to work on the same critical issue or policy.[12]

PRACTICAL SOLUTIONS

Those who disagree on political issues can reduce the potential for conflict by finding ways to work together in the political arena. One possibility is voter registration drives. All church members should have the opportunity to exercise their right to vote by becoming registered voters. Pastors can create multichurch registration coalitions, supported by the NAACP,[13] to increase community voting power.

In addition, each community has specific needs—transportation, environmental safety and equity, community violence—that require sustained political attention throughout the year. Churches can develop their own non-profit corporations or work with established groups to politically educate the pew about how legislative funds are made available to communities to address specific concerns, how bills get to state legislatures, and what impact directed community-based political action can have.

Finally, the *African American Heritage Hymnal* provides useful litanies designed to assist churches in the encouragement of togetherness in this arena. In particular, see Unity (#49) and Peace (#37).

PROGRAMS AND PREMISES

Local NAACP historians will come to teach brief classes at one or several churches that share a collective learning goal. Individuals can also learn political history through detailed information available on the NAACP website.[14] *Eyes on the Prize*, both the book and the film, can be used to teach political history in the same manner. See Appendix E—Recommended Resources for additional materials.

PASTORAL MANAGEMENT

Political topics often create chasms that divide those who otherwise share a belief in Christ. Pastors, too, may fall into a particular political camp. As a result, pastoral management can determine to approach issues in the political arena in a number of ways: (1) Only take a believer's stance based on Scripture. (2) Work as a conciliator regardless of the political stance of parishioners. (3) Use sermons to judiciously discuss practical issues, connecting current issues to those represented in Scripture. (4) Bring in an outside group or facilitator to bridge the divide. Conflicts that are potentially intractable tend to bring out our primal (infantile and animalistic) responses.

PROMISES

Thinking about the Civil War's end and how best to care for all of those affected by slavery, Abraham Lincoln ended his second inaugural speech with a thought that invoked God's support for the country's good works on the Master's behalf:

> With malice toward none, with charity for all, with firmness in the right as God gives us to see the right, let us strive on to finish the work we are in, ... to do all which may achieve and cherish a just and lasting peace among ourselves and with all nations.[15]

Such acts give those who seek a just and lasting peace the promise of a future in which God sits firmly at the center. The human beings who serve God, no matter their many labels, are then not confused about their roles in the Lord's service. Diminished conflict (no red or blue states) clears the path to Christ.

taking off the shackles

Is it difficult for you to have a calm discussion with those with whom you disagree politically? If so, why? If not, why not?

How can the followers of Jesus live out our faith so that the teachings of Jesus are not trivialized by political operatives seeking to traffic on his message in the name of their partisan (Republican/red versus Democrat/blue or otherwise) political aims rather than the transcendent, redemptive purposes of God? Though we, of course, cannot know his viewpoint with certainty, what opinions can you suggest based on what Jesus said or did in reaction or response to similar controversies and disagreements in his day?

Do African American Christians believe in the separation of church and state? Should we? How is it demonstrated? How does it protect our churches and our rights? At home, in our schools?

Do you consider *liberal* to be a bad word? Why or why not? If so, why and what must be done to clean it up and once again make it respectable? Which political party (Democrats or Republicans) made it distasteful? How did each side accomplish the sullying of the word?

What is your political identity and why? Is it based on your African-ness, American-ness, Christian-ness, or other self-defined status?

Our ancestors died to make politics safe for us. Are there political issues—the right to do X—for which you would die? Are there ways that you are living that improve options (this, too, is political) for your children and/or community?

Do claims that America is "a Christian nation" contribute to a sense of national self-righteousness, if not clericalism or possible creation of a theocracy? How can individual believers, local congregations, and religious entities act so these tendencies are avoided and resisted?

10

nondenominationalism

"But the hour is coming, and is now here,
when the true worshipers will worship the Father in spirit and
truth, for the Father seeks such as these to worship him."
—John 4:23, NRSV

INCREASINGLY THE END OF THE TWENTIETH AND THE BEGINNING OF
the twenty-first centuries have seen America's churches move away
from traditional denominational labels to become "Christian
Centers," "Faith Temples," "New Testament," or other nondenominational churches. What are the reasons for this trend in general?
Because denominational African American churches have strengthened
and solidified so many components of the community throughout our
American history, does the church lose essential components of its special identity ("How I got over!") if it loses the names, dogma, and rites
of the seven traditional African American denominations?

When I trained as a deacon, I had an interesting discussion with my
pastor about just this topic and the challenges it was causing in the
black church. Understanding how proud I am to be Baptist and how
concerned I was that denominational traditions might be lost (which
was part of my reason for writing *Total Praise: An Orientation to
Black Baptist Belief and Worship*), he, a proud Baptist pastor, noted
that among the strengths of nondenominational churches is that they
"are forced to consider their beliefs and to find ways to sustain those
beliefs while at the same time encouraging creativity and new avenues
for faith and work. After all, the salvation of the church is not in its
structure but in the One who called the church into being. Breaking
away from structure is not all bad."[1]

This was an excellent response as it pertains to nondenominational churches that were specifically designed to support strong Christian beliefs, rather than theology and dogma, which was the genesis of my question.[2] Though theology will, of course, be taught, not all of our nondenominational churches form with this as their initial primary goal. When churches form from "congregational splits" or as a result of "power grabs," as is occasionally the case, faith tenets may be secondary to other more human objectives.

T. M. Robinson maintains that nondenominationalism has taken away from the strength of established denominations. Worried that those who did not know their denominational history and beliefs could easily lose their traditions, he wrote an article titled "The Farce of Nondenominationalism," in which the word was defined in its strictest sense:

> "Non-denominational" literally means "no value" or "no standard." To denominate something is to designate a nomenclature, name, or label representative of that value or standard. Hence, a denomination is a name representing a value or standard. For example, consider dollar bills. When asked what denominations are in your wallet, the question is asking you to state the value that each dollar bill represents. Of course, a five dollar denomination does not represent the same value or standard as a hundred dollar denomination. Likewise, after stating their doctrinal beliefs fully, most churches will match denominational labels representing those unique beliefs. Rejecting all labeling goes against the godly examples given in Scripture. Therefore, having such a wealth of church history to draw upon, a truly nondenominational church would be a church that doesn't believe anything strong enough to earn itself a label.[3]

While this viewpoint is one that extrapolates from the dictionary definition of *nondenominational*, it does not go terribly far in delineating its emotional meaning to the believer. Responding to the conflict created by the article that described nondenominational as farcical, the Reverend Richard Gruhn wrote the following:

> To see the fading of traditional denominational lines is truly remarkable and healthy. Christians of almost every stripe are looking for a church or a minister who meets their needs. Nondenominationalism is not a farce, nor is it a cult. It is the body of Christ (Christians born again) doing the work of the Lord, leading sinners to eternal life in Jesus Christ....The oneness of God which holds no denominational title is beautiful.[4]

Is the answer to this conflict so simple among African American Christians? Is beauty gained if, in the goal of the oneness that the Rev. Gruhn describes, the rich tradition of Richard Allen in the AME Church[5] or Quassey among Baptists[6] could potentially be lost? Does one goal necessarily preclude the other?

There are important socioeconomic reasons for the trend away from denominational power in recent years, including:

Demographic shifts. Since the Industrial Revolution of 1870,[7] the United States has seen demographic population shifts from rural farming to urban industrial to technology-related (computer to Internet-driven employment sectors). African Americans, impacted by two such shifts, moved south to north between 1915–1940.

Denominational declines. Nationally, Protestant churches are having difficulty filling their ranks, including those of pastors who may not wish to be assigned to out-of-the-way churches with small salaries, and especially those in locations with limited career opportunities for their spouses. According to Peter Smith, religion journalist for the *Courier-Journal* of Louisville, Kentucky, and author of a series of articles on why the nation's pulpits are emptying, "While some church officials laud the influx of career changers bringing real-world experience to the pulpit, others say incoming seminarians have lower academic credentials than in the past and often arrive with low levels of religious literacy and with high personal and therapeutic needs."[8] Church dissension, combined with low pay and long hours, is "chewing up and spitting out wonderful people of God," said a 1999 study in, the Lutheran Church–Missouri Synod.[9] Larger churches in cities were noted to be able to find pastors, though many problems faced by denominations were the same.

Denominational schisms. Shifts away from denominations have most often been for reasons of personal ambition and politics than because of theological or dogmatic concerns. Among National Baptists, denominational schisms occurred in 1915[10] over the control of the publishing board, then in 1961, as earlier noted, regarding the political activity of the Rev. Martin Luther King Jr.

Church splits. Churches split in the African American community for a number of reasons, among which are pastoral ego and conflicts regarding the specifics of Christian belief. Nondenominational churches often form from these splits, giving the churches and the pastors opportunities for new identities and fresh starts. What can often be lost in the transition, though (unless the pastor makes clear in the written details provided from the previous church history), is archival continuity from the old to the new church. In those cases, unless a senior saint is available to tell the story, or a church or community historian can piece it together, essential history, both of the church and of individuals within the church, might be irretrievably lost.[11]

Nepotistic needs. In some cases, fed mainly by pastoral ego, nondenominational churches can form as a result of pastors who wish to start their own churches specifically so that they will have no accountability to church, denominational, or other hierarchical entities. While many highly reputable persons pastor nondenominational congregations, others fear that there is a risk that, if one co-pastors with a spouse, and the church office is run by a family member, very few persons among the lay leadership of the church are going to feel comfortable standing up to policies that the pastor and his or her family establishes. Nepotistic systems create structures in which no one can easily tell family members the truth for fear of reprisal. In cases where the family in charge has set up clear systems of accountability and makes it clear that they are potentially fallible, the management structure can work as well as other systems. The church—nondenominational or otherwise—whose purpose is to establish the pastor as a demigod is on a constant path of conflict. The church whose purpose is to work on behalf of Christ with the pastor as an accountable servant among servants will function effectively and with minimal conflict.

Dogmatic discernment. Concerns that one's established denomination is not meeting the needs of the local congregation and, because of political or ethical problems at the top, will not be able to do so, can be an important reason for choosing nondenominationalism over traditional groups.

Heaven only knows. There is no data available on why most pastors or churches that make the nondenominational choice do so. Ask preachers at any denominational convention, though, and they will tell you that nondenominationalism is a trend. Anecdotally, it appears that many churches that make the choice to become nondenominational maintain the dogma of their initial denomination—for example, AME or Baptist teachings—without using the official name. Often it is unclear exactly why the choice for nondenominational status was made, though it can sometimes be inferred. In some cases, for example, female pastors who might not have been able to advance in leadership capacities in their home or adopted churches started their own congregations; men who wished to become bishops in denominations that did not have bishopric hierarchies shifted structures or developed new ones; sons of successful pastor-fathers struck out on their own without their paternal shadows; or pastoral couples began successful Bible ministries that progressed into formats outside of easily recognized denominational structures and continued to explore Christ through innovative media formats over which they could exercise entrepreneurial control.

Nondenominational (independent) churches or congregations total 4 percent of American Christian houses of worship.[12] Notable nondenominational congregations include The Potters House, led by Bishop T. D. Jakes. Jakes is also an author, actor, playwright, songwriter, and supporter of abused women. Another influential nondenominational pastor is the Rev. Dr. Creflo Dollar of the World Changers Church International.

Dollar began in the AME Church, suffered an injury that thwarted football goals, studied psychology and history in college, was ordained a Baptist minister, and, with his wife, turned a small Bible study group into a small nondenominational church that has grown into a multi-million dollar multimedia group of which he is the CEO and pastor.[13]

To make a decision about whether staying within a denomination is desirable or not, one must weigh a variety of factors. The short-term impacts of nondenominationalism include the loss of fellowship with other churches within the denomination, association, or convention, and the inputs and benefits that are attained through those relationships. The long-term impacts related to congregational stability of the local church are the capacity of conventions to assist smaller churches in kingdom-building ventures. Yet another benefit of denominational relationships is the collective strength and wisdom that comes from these relationships. Elijah, it is said, might have complained from his dried-up brook that he was alone in his ministry not merely because Ahab and Jezebel despised and threatened him, but because he was not part of a fellowship (see 1 Kings 19:1-9). Because nondenominational churches tend to be ships unto themselves, it is not clear the degree to which they learn lessons of fellowship from one another.

The dynamics of potential conflict related to becoming a nondenominational church are similar to those involved in a church move. Indeed, the church is moving in some sense, though it is not a physical move. It is important to found independent churches in a way that creates minimal conflict between and among pastors, lay leaders, parishioners, and denominational entities. A new temple for Christ should be a matter of excitement for everyone but the devil.

the 8 p's

The discussion about denominationalism versus nondenominationalism often has less to do with Christ than with the label we place on how to praise him. When we evaluate the legitimate conflicts that occasionally emerge regarding the issue, no matter which side of the issue we are on, we must ask ourselves several important questions:

■ Are my concerns a matter of truth or taste? Paul asked us to speak the truth in love rather than to force our preferences on another.

■ Does the difference I am concerned about regarding denominationalism actually matter? If it does, then prayerfully, how shall I make it known?

■ Am I trusting the Holy Spirit in this or acting out something more personal in my quest?

For many, it is important to maintain a connection to the denominational church and its historical traditions, strengthening them, learning from and worshiping within their tenets and dogmatic structures. Others believe that Christ and African American traditions can coexist in nondenominational church structures if their organizations are carefully honed and their beliefs and hierarchies are not charismatically, egotiscally, and/or nepotistically designed.

Let's delve further now into the 8 P's to direct us in the process of getting to Amen.

PRAYER

To begin something new requires stepping out on faith in a profound way, one that, dependent on motivation, will either be cause for rejoicing or will be terribly misunderstood. This prayer by Vienna Cobb Anderson, focused on the conflicts and the challenge of the decisions faced by Christ's mother, Mary, brings hope and peace. Mary's prayer can also be ours, as we ask that we become brave enough to risk taking big steps, crossing closed barriers, or opening our hearts to the unexpected.

PRAYER FOR THE COURAGE TO TAKE RISKS

Mary, you heard a voice. You answered, "Yes,"
    risking shame and disgrace, ridicule and rejection.
Still, you said, "Yes." Yes, to the promise you received from God.
Yes, to the birth of a firstborn son. Let your trust be
    our inspiration,

your faith be our guide, your hope our course for courage.
This we ask
in the name of the child you bore, the Savior of the world,
who came
through God's abiding love and your spoken word.
Yes. So be it. Amen.[14]

PREACHING
After Jesus had fasted in the desert for forty days and nights, he told the tempter who came to him, "It is written: 'Man does not live on bread alone, but on every word that comes from the mouth of God'" (Matthew 4:4, NIV). Preachers, taking any of Christ's words, can feed his people in temples of any name.

PARISHIONER AWARENESS
When a church is breaking away from a traditional African American denomination to form a nondenominational congregation, all steps established by the denomination for such breaks should be followed, laying out for congregants the clear strengths and weaknesses of each denomination and nondenominationalism. In either case, but especially important for those starting from the ground up, having followed a pattern of growth from an anointed son or daughter of God, the issues that must be addressed have to do with the degree to which the church has the economic wherewithal, managerial support, and organizational infrastructure required for survival.

People in the pews want to know what is happening in their churches. Making sure they are well informed will decrease gossip and infighting among leaders and will limit dissension in the ranks regarding how temples are formed.

PERSPECTIVE(S) ON PROBLEMS
Once the negative concerns of pastoral ego (and the resulting attendant cult of charisma), nepotism, and the potential for insular structure have been addressed in nondenominational structures, how a church is

denominationally organized may be less important than how it is developed as an environment in which Christ can be effectively glorified. Remembering that the church is "one body in Christ" is a helpful tool for conflict management. Author Peter Steinke tells us, "When we think of the congregation as a system or a whole, we also consider all of the interactions of the parts—and the emotional environment in which those interactions take place. What interactions most support health? What emotional interactions most encourage disease process? Is the emotional environment leading toward health or illness?"[15]

In other cases where churches face potential conflict resulting from a proposed shift in church denominational structure, it is important to assess the reasons that the church became nondenominational (i.e., pastor and parishioners must examine whether the shift from denominational to nondenominational structure is for Christian purpose rather than human purposes). In these cases, working through problems must take a more interpersonal approach. Daneen Skube, syndicated columnist on interpersonal issues in the marketplace (which is the corporate structure more similar to how many new nondenominational churches are organized) states that "power struggles are a common emotional agenda for meetings. Trying to get (other people) to admit that they are (creating conflict) won't work; they'll (all) just fight with you. Instead, appeal to the group's need to get work done. Realize that power struggles in meetings can represent unresolved conflicts in the organization."[16]

If a congregation prayerfully decides to become nondenominational, then such a shift is an act that holds within it doctrinal integrity. It is important to found independent churches in a way that creates minimal conflict between pastors, lay leaders, parishioners (denominational groups, when this occurs), and the community. A new temple for Christ should be a matter of excitement for everyone but the devil.

PRACTICAL SOLUTIONS

It may be advisable for churches to hire strategists to assist them with short- and long-term organizational, financial, and succession planning.

Because nondenominational churches are often founded by their pastors, it is essential that they plan for survival past the life of the pastor. Many Christian management firms exist in large cities to help with organizational planning. Those in small cities can get assistance from business departments at community colleges or can use Christian management software designed for this purpose.

PROGRAMS AND PREMISES
Nondenominationalism broadens our thinking beyond the guidelines set within denominations. It asks us to reach across traditional borders, which is often uncomfortable, for the sake of the growth of Christ's church.

PASTORAL MANAGEMENT
If nondenominationalism represents a new language of faith, then it may also signify a new way of thinking about pastoral management within its new context.

> Every Tuesday morning at the World Changers campus, [Dr. Creflo] Dollar gathers his senior managers for a cabinet meeting. At World Changers, there are no problems, only "challenges," and the cheerful, energetic inhabitants have turned professionalism…into a ruling ideology. Dollar is an "excellence nut."…Like most of the church's initiatives, (the Lost Sheep Ministry) was a sophisticated exercise in consumer marketing. The ministry was to target three thousand dropouts, each of whom would receive a letter with an invitation to rejoin the flock, followed by a phone call, and then, if necessary, a visit from a ministry delegate… Dollar…had to wonder whether the church might have done more to help them, and keep their *business*.[17]

More than just souls to save, this new perception of the congregant as currency may cause conflict within the church. Pastors, in bringing in souls through new management ideas, must be ever-sensitive to the tension between the old and the new. The historic, the present, and the future needs of the church are a sensitive and essential mathematical calculus that are ever-present in the life of the African American church. Church leadership must be aware of them, understanding that, dependent on a variety of social and environmental factors, each will shift, varying its relative importance during specific moments in time. Assessment then, becomes an important part of any decision-making process regarding denominational structure, as does transparency and communication between leadership and members of the congregation. Conflict diminished when communication is open regarding the balance between shifting historical factors related to church and community, evaluation processes will be agreed upon, if appropriate, and outcomes will be discussed with the congregation.

PROMISES

If denominational churches are losing pastors, then the mainline denominations must work to strengthen themselves. Nondenominational churches, for their part, must assure their longevity by not being cults of personality or of the prosperity gospel. They must develop infrastructures that can live beyond the influence of those who start them and attract parishioners, funds, and programs. The promise for the church is that, together, lives can be changed, communities can be enriched, and the mission of the church can be lived.

taking off the shackles

What are areas of ministry focus that black religious bodies/denominations might pursue jointly? What impediments prevent them from exploring those possibilities? How might those impediments be resolved and by whom? What are you prepared to do to support such joint efforts?

What are some ways that conventions and denominations present or modify their policies into ministries that strengthen the ways local congregations relate to people? Might conventions and denominations have a difficult time translating their policies into useful programs that meaningfully affect the life of the local church? If the AME, AMEZ, CME, COGIC, or the several NBC conventions run the risk of getting bogged down in their own workings, might it not be best to become nondenominational and freed of those structures?

Is nondenominationalism preferable to the existing array of black religious bodies? Is there any reason to believe that the factors and forces that contributed toward the creation and maintenance of different denominations are less present than they were when the various bodies were formed? Or is nondenominationalism just another denomination without a name?

How is doctrinal structure, theological integrity, and mission responsibility determined and validated among nondenominational religious bodies? Who determines and validates them? Do denominations sustain models of ministry that are outdated?

How is the temptation toward personality cultism different within denominational bodies than for congregations associated with denominations or conventions? How does one protect against this? How do churches with charismatic pastors do succession planning?

Does it matter what the organization is called so long as, in it, Christ is glorified, souls are saved, and missions are engaged?

going forward from here

11

why god don't like ugly: proposing a collaborative future

> "Blessed are the peacemakers, for they
> will be called children of God."
> —Matthew 5:9, NRSV

G ETTING TO AMEN IS, TO BE SURE, A CHALLENGING PROCESS. THESE closing chapters and the appendices that follow look toward the future with an eye toward continuing the process this book has hopefully begun. The goal is to give direction to provide healing through a range of specific activities, starting at the local church level and reaching throughout the African diaspora.

As a whole generation of grandmothers has been known to say, "God don't like ugly," and ugly is what our history of the conflicts discussed in this book has sometimes become. Though aspects of conflict can be healthy and can assist us in a process of personal and church growth, the African American church has often engaged conflicts in a negative manner. As a conflict-management strategy that can be flexibly applied, the 8 P's take us from Prayers to Promises so that we might actively create and support a positive future.

what the black church faces

In 1899, poet Rudyard Kipling wrote a poem entitled "The White Man's Burden," which strongly influenced and provided literary support for the imperialist posture of England and the United States. Instructing superior whites to "take up" the "burden" (suspected to be virtually impossible) of improving the naturally bleak lot of blacks, called the "half-devil and half-child,"[1] Kipling's poem reflected and gave increased license to an already pervasive set of racist views held by imperialists. It additionally angered notable leaders of the AME Church, who as editors of the AME newspaper, *The Recorder*, declared the poem to be "unquestionably a verse license to injustice and tribute to Caucasian avarice and cruelty such as has no parallel in any mad flight of the poetic muse."[2] To further make their point that imperial whites required the forgiveness of the very God they used as justification for their actions against people of color, *The Recorder*'s editors responded in verse, using the format and cadence of Kipling's poem:

Pile on the Black Man's Burden
His wail with laughter drown
You've sealed the Red Man's problem,
And will take up the Brown,
In vain you seek to end it,
With bullet, blood or death
Better far to defend it
With honor's holy breath.[3]

Certainly, African Americans have borne the burdens of organized oppression resulting from imperialist philosophies and pervasive scientific beliefs that viewed us as inferior. From this oppression, African American churches were created in defiance of laws that sought to subjugate us and the societal structures that reinforced beliefs that pushed us against the wall, held us to unreasonable standards, made us fight for the rights promised us as persons living under the provisions of the Constitution, and even with new laws on the books, flouted them, often placing us on the defensive.

Defensive postures are well known to psychologists and other social scientists. As frequently as it calls forth the urge to vigorously and vocally defend oneself against untruths, the half-life of oppression is often self-doubt and self-hatred. Oppressed persons become victims of the negative perceptions held by their oppressors. They learn to view themselves as others have viewed them and to behave in a manner that makes it difficult to move beyond what rapidly becomes a negative group stereotype. This defensive, self-hating stance is the ultimate goal of oppressors, to keep people enslaved long after the shackles have been removed.

To the degree that we suffer from post-slavery trauma—an extended communal form of traumatic stress—we have not grieved slavery, America has not apologized for it, and we carry painful, heavy loads. Healing these wounds is essential, and it requires deliberate action through the collective efforts of black churches and communities. appendices B–D suggest ideas and strategies for developing annual calendars of shared cultural and communal experiences that allow us, across denominations, to process our pain, claim our history, and in so doing, make good on the eighth P, Promises, as a way to create and sustain our future.

As a place for healing and hope, the black church has always purposefully sought to move its people beyond defensive postures. In a twenty-first century that has politicized Christianity, we may also be required to refocus our theology, enhance our faith in the God who has faith in us, and strengthen our avenues for achieving individual and community economic stability, educational excellence, employment opportunity, and the strengthening of our collective emotional reserves. As our strongest social institutions, our churches must also work together to create an interdenominational network designed to make the African American church as a whole more than a number of local churches with different histories and organizational structures. We must work together to combat the crisis of church and community conflict. We must fashion our own *diaspora by design*: an organized system of services and support that we create, implement, manage, and monitor. It should be our goal to be a cross-denominational stronghold that supports the development of community leaders, local and national businesses, academic institutions, and community-serving organizations that facilitate our capacity to be our own harbors, domestic and global, in the best of times and in our times of storm. With our hearts, souls, spirits, minds, tithes, time, energy, and determination, we must succeed in our efforts to build God's church in his name and for his sake.

where the black church stands

This is where we stand—in the bright sunshine of triumph for our daily accomplishments and our awareness of what we have come through and have overcome.

This is where we stand—on the shores of a land that enslaved us, terrorized us, legislated against us, and refuses to apologize to us.

This is where we stand—on planet Earth, in the shifting sands of time.

This is where we stand—on God's Word and under his cross.

12

reclaiming the tribe: taking off the shackles in jesus' name

Come on people now!
Smile on your brother
Everybody get together
Try to love one another
Right now![1]

removing the shackles

THIS MANTRA-LIKE SONG OF THE 1960s BY THE YOUNGBLOODS exemplifies another era and a different approach to love and to living. It makes very good Christian sense to look on our brothers and sisters with love, putting differences aside and *trying* to love one another, even though the task may sometimes be difficult. The American fiction, after all, is that love is an easy thing. This self-same fiction is why our culture suffers from such a high divorce rate: no one seems to understand that love takes work, love hurts, and love is a process that has wonderful rewards.

Love is also what helps us work through our conflicts. The African American church and community have myriad challenges, but there is a very real truth: we need to stop fighting each other and turn those energies outward toward the issues that negatively impact us. To do our ministry well, inside the church and outside its walls, we must address the issues that challenge the larger church of Christ, and, because charity begins at home, we must start with the African American church.

Taking off our shackles requires an honest look at our very real flaws. It requires answering questions, those posed in the chapters of this book, and those we know that arise from living our lives. This book has presented a model and has discussed some specific issues in detail. These issues were selected because they appeared to be at the top of the list of issues that our churches dealt with poorly. There are other issues that cause conflict within our churches to be sure. The purpose of this book is to help us walk through a process of understanding why we are where we are in the conflict-resolution process and to acknowledge that getting to Amen may shift based on the particular issue we choose to address.

looking toward future options

Collectively, our next step must involve looking to the future. Such a step is an opportunity to, among other options:

■ cross denominational boundaries and create partnerships never before imagined;

■ through models forwarded by African American churches, stop the language of victimization;

■ work with successful African American businesspersons to discuss means of harnessing our economic power into jobs and businesses; and

■ create, enhance, build, and grow African American churches that reflect our history and make them shout out loud while taking us into a new century.

As a piece of art and history that created a bridge between the past and present, the *Negro National Anthem* was remarkably prescient in its scope. Written in 1899 by James Weldon Johnson, it pulls from the past while imagining the future, something that African Americans must also do as part of the process of creating community, managing conflict, and planning for a collaborative future.

THE NEGRO NATIONAL ANTHEM
The past
Lift every voice and sing
Till earth and heaven ring,

Ring with the harmonies of Liberty;
Let our rejoicing rise
High as the listening skies,
Let it resound loud as the rolling sea.
Sing a song full of the faith that the dark past has taught us,
Sing a song full of the hope that the present has brought us,
Facing the rising sun of our new day begun
Let us march on till victory is won.

The challenge that moves us past conflict
Stony the road we trod,
Bitter the chastening rod,
Felt in the days when hope unborn had died;
Yet with a steady beat,
Have not our weary feet
Come to the place for which our fathers sighed?
We have come over a way that with tears have been watered,
We have come, treading our path through the blood of the
  slaughtered,
Out from the gloomy past,
Till now we stand at last
Where the white gleam of our bright star is cast.

The promise
God of our weary years,
God of our silent tears,
Thou who hast brought us thus far on the way;
Thou who hast by Thy might
Led us into the light,
Keep us forever in the path, we pray.
Lest our feet stray from the places, Our God, where we met
  Thee;
Lest, our hearts drunk with the wine of the world, we forget
  Thee;

Shadowed beneath Thy hand,
May we forever stand.
True to our GOD,
True to our native land.

The importance of the *Negro National Anthem* in the twenty-first
century is that it so beautifully illuminates what the African American
church must do to create healthy communities that successfully manage
conflict and, more important, work to establish a vision that builds on
our history to step into a strong, faith-centered, economically and edu-
cationally viable future. The church can take leadership of this effort,
partnering with other traditionally strong and dedicated black organizations (such as the NAACP) and successful individuals who share the
vision. Seeing the shackles that once bound us, the anthem also envisions
those shackles victoriously removed in a future where we, with God's
help, walk an enlightened path. To get there requires a whole slew of
Amens; a sense of humility that allows us to acknowledge the baggage
that we (individually and organizationally) take into any room that contributes to conflict; a determination to throw away the role of victim; a
promise to ask hard questions of ourselves; a love of each other and
Christ that allows us to use the tools of conflict management to work
through the petty and meaningless to get to the important goals that can
help us, with a plan, to build the Kingdom.

taking care with the answers

Stepping into his new future, Tom Brokaw signed off as anchor of
NBC's *Nightly News* on December 1, 2004, ending the broadcast by
making a brief statement about his two decades as a newsman. In
every port of call in which he found himself around the world, people
shared joys, demonstrated bravery, or behaved in ways that ranged
from confusing to abominable. His voice cracking with emotion,
Brokaw offered a tremendous insight about a world currently in conflict and how we must think about healing it. "It's not the questions

that get us in trouble," he said. "It's the answers."

It is always what we pick based on what we know that demonstrates whether we have chosen our way or God's way. Ultimately, knowing the difference between those two essential paths—and knowing that sometimes only God has all the answers—is what effective conflict management is about. To get to Amen we must:

Pray without ceasing.

Believe fervently.

Question intently.

Listen carefully.

Enter humbly.

Love one another openly, especially if it feels difficult.

And ask Jehovah Shalom, the God of peace, to live in our hearts and guide our paths.

appendix A
case study: conflict between the pastor and another church leader

by Rev. Wendell L. Griffen, Coordinator of Ministries, Mount Pleasant Baptist Church, Little Rock, Arkansas, and Parliamentarian, National Baptist Convention, USA, Inc.

THE TERM *PASTOR* OFTEN EVOKES PLEASANT THOUGHTS OF AN understanding and patient soul who stands with us during times of crisis, calms us in times of confusion, counsels us in times of indecision and anxiety, and exhorts us with the triumphant assurances that God loves us and is calling us to live to his glory in the power of the Holy Spirit. At the same time, the pastoral function can also involve conflict with other church leaders.

During my pastoral service at another congregation, I became sensitized about the high level of chronic illness within the membership and our surrounding community. Cardiovascular disease, diabetes, poor dental care, obesity, and a host of other factors were robbing God's people of the vitality they needed to nurture families, work, serve one another, and live triumphantly. When a local hospital approached me about forming a partnership for congregational health ministry, I quickly accepted the opportunity. The arrangement called for the hospital to help locate health care professionals and services for screening and education purposes. These services were provided without cost. Our congregation rejoiced about the opportunity.

The key to the ministry initiative depended on providing access to the screening and educational resources when people would take advantage of them. Our congregational health care team concluded that our best chance for reaching people with the health and wellness services and information would be on Sunday, when more people intentionally were present. The team recommended that we devote one Sunday each month to screening and education after morning worship and provide an education period during the Sunday school time slot.

Our Sunday school staff accepted the proposal without disagreement, with the exception of one teacher, who refused to dismiss her class to attend the health and wellness education sessions. I tried to reason with the objecting teacher (who suffered from some health issues that included hypertension and whose class members suffered from some chronic conditions that they desperately needed help understanding and treating). She insisted that it was wrong to devote Sunday school time for health and wellness education. I preached sermons about Jesus and his healing ministry. I met privately with the teacher in an effort to personally enlist her compliance with what the rest of the adult department was doing regarding health and wellness. Nothing worked. When the health and wellness sessions occurred each month, this teacher refused to dismiss her class so her students could attend. The students, unwilling to appear rude or disrespectful, remained in the class and were denied access to information needed to help them be healthier.

Eventually, I dismissed the teacher from the class after concluding that her students deserved the chance to learn how to be good stewards of their bodies, even during Sunday school time once a month, whether she was teacher or not. She left the congregation. The health and wellness ministry continued and worked to improve health for persons in the congregation as well as provide access to health information and screening for the neighborhood around the church. I learned many important things from this experience:

Pastoral leadership sometimes leads to conflicts with other congregational leaders. I knew this truth cognitively, but my experience with the Sunday school teacher involving our health and wellness ministry made that truth personal and painful.

Pastoral conflicts with other church leaders involving ministry initiatives carry significant risks. Our conflict challenged more than a working relationship between a teacher and the pastor; it challenged our personal fellowship as well. Although the teacher and I remained cordial toward each other during and after the conflict, other teachers and leaders in the adult Sunday school department knew that the teacher was defying what the rest of the congregation had agreed to do. I needed to address the situation.

At some point, the pastor must take a stand. I eventually had to decide whether or not to ignore the defiant teacher and allow her to prevent her students from benefiting from what our congregation had affirmed as a ministry initiative in health and wellness. This problem could not be delegated to others. I was unwilling to ignore the defiance. I attended too many sick rooms and funerals of members whose diseases led to untimely deaths because they either did not know how to care for themselves or lacked the supportive encouragement from others in the congregation regarding eating habits, exercise, weight control, etc. That experience strengthened my sense of moral and spiritual responsibility to confront any force that might deny health and wellness information and resources to the people God entrusted to my care.

I regret that the conflict resulted in losing the teacher. I do not regret making the stand. **The people we reached were worth the teacher we lost.** I suppose conflict resolution ultimately turns, at some level, on a form of cost-benefit analysis. Sooner or later, we must decide whether the benefits perceived in effecting a given course of action to resolve a conflict outweigh the cost that will ensue from the conflict and the way it is resolved.

God's grace is sovereign, not our conflicts. During the time I was dealing with the defiant teacher, our conflict seemed very dominant in my ministry and in the health and wellness ministry initiative. But it was not. The conflict was important, but it was not sovereign. Our health and wellness ministry team was saddened by the conflict and disappointed that the teacher refused to cooperate. However, we sensed that God's will was bigger than the conflict. Indeed, we eventually realized that God's will for us involved moving through the conflict to new ministry opportunities and challenges for the health and wellness ministry.

appendix B
suggested coordinated local activities

A S HAS BEEN STRESSED THROUGHOUT *GETTING TO AMEN*, AN IM-portant component of solving conflicts as well as of manag-ing them long term is an essential P, Programs and Premises. Programs and Premises focuses on designing programs whose pur-pose is to address the issues that caused the conflict among church members in a manner that allows those on both sides of the conflict to benefit from what has been learned in its resolution.

To successfully get from Prayer to Promises requires that individual churches be willing to step out on faith, certainly the faith of the convictions that may have influenced the initial conflict, but also a faith that acknowl-edges the vulnerability of growing beyond being wrong in some cases.

This specific agenda and calendar asks individual churches to work together, coordinating their Programs and Premises to provide strategic services and target needs impossible for one church alone to manage. It recommends that the local churches in a community consider an agenda of coordinated activities, samples of which are below. While these samples are a stepping-off point, churches will, through an assess-ment process, arrive at their own list of local community needs. Guiding principles for the local activities include evaluating church resources to address identified issues and aligning program needs with missions of the local church and the Great Commission.

agenda
Multidenominational church board. Create denominational and cross-denominational alliance boards to provide an array of services within the local community. This board, which can coordinate serv-ices and ideas generated by local church boards, will require

coordinated fund-raising through grant writing (experts are available in each congregation), dinners, and creative ventures. Develop a board-specific mission and vision. Practice conflict-neutral strategies to get work accomplished.

Social service alliances. Provide support services to community members who require them. This is of particular assistance to small churches that may not have sufficient members or funds to do this work on their own. Most important, however, by creating the alliances, those who need services get them, and denominations, many of whom are not used to working together, grow from the effort, from the leadership down.

Coordinated missions. Develop a coordinated Church Mission Day, the purpose of which is to collect funds for domestic and foreign ministries on topics whose cycles rotate (education, health, women's programs, children's programs, housing, environment, arts, recreation, technology, and infrastructure) based on a decision process decided upon by a cross-denominational leadership council. The leadership should rotate between denominations (seven-year cycles)[1] and leadership should be broadly defined between pulpit and lay leaders. Local churches in the community can also work on coordinated international missions (see Appendix D), as well as to plan individually to travel as a group, both of which activities should be coordinated by the multidenominational church board.

Conflict management council. Create a council that provides creative training for local churches in conflict management. This training can be provided by regional, national, or local groups knowledgeable about working in the black community (see Appendix E). Over time they can help community churches become experts who can "train the trainers" in effective conflict management methodology for use in solving church crises and long-term problems. The eventual goal can be the development of an African American Christian Conflict Management training resource owned and operated by members of the African American community that could be used by our churches, members of our community, and all others in need of its services.

calendar

African-centered activities. Churches can work with local community organizations to coordinate local activities such as Juneteenth. At Christmas, a Christ-Kwanzaa celebration, either sponsored by the church coalition in a local community center, or rotating each value to one of the churches participating in the coalition, can be a special gift to the local community.

Arts. An annual arts festival, black film festival, or a production such as Langston Hughes's Black Nativity can be coordinated through the multidenominational church council. Funds raised can be used to create a community-based scholarship fund for college students.

appendix C
suggested coordinated national activities

T O MOVE FROM PRAYER TO PROMISES, IT IS RECOMMENDED THAT the traditionally black denominations consider the coordination of their efforts in the development of a cross-denominational national foundation (to be named through a process that will engage the conflict management skills of those involved in its development). The calendar and agenda suggested in appendix B recommended that local churches coordinate their efforts to provide a mechanism by which social services, in which individual churches might engage, could be exponentially increased through a church network that facilitated personnel and funding resources, services focused on enhancing community values, and the arts.

This appendix recommends a national foundation in which the focus expands similar ideas to the national arena. The principles underlying this national foundation will include guidelines, across denominations, for enacting action plans based on considerations for structuring reasonable expectations for the work of a national foundation; coordinating denominational personnel and financial resources to facilitate the work of a national foundation; assessing national (regional) church community needs for potential programs of a national foundation; and determining short- and long-term plans of a national foundation.

agenda

The recommended agenda of the cross-denominational national foundation is to create multiple ways of maintaining the history of the traditionally African American denominations, to conduct research on African American faith patterns, and to support leaders in the faith through:

Creating a library to preserve the history of the traditionally African American denominations. (To the degree that each has its own manner of doing so, information can be strategically shared with the foundation.) The black church is strengthened by the creation of a common resource that respects and reflects our history, acknowledges our strengths, places its weaknesses in context, and celebrates our perseverance.

Honoring African American pastoral and theological giants through awards and documentary works. In 2004, the Hampton University Ministers' Conference began a Living Legends Awards program. The foundation may determine to have books written about each legend, adding these written documents to their library. They may also arrive at other innovative ideas for honoring these and other legends whose lives and works have been noted as essential to the growth of the African American church.

Developing a program of research on African American churches (denominational and nondenominational), of the faith patterns of African American persons and of African persons of faith across the diaspora. Sites such as www.barna.com have excellent information, and www.alban.org provided survey assessment tools, but having African American Christian owned and operated sites with the same resources would be an excellent addition to the available data pool. It should be part of the mission of the research agendas of such groups that they remain staunchly nonpartisan.

Producing a State of the Faith annual publication that details research findings. Data sources can be gleaned from the recommended African American data sites, aided by research collected at local levels through surveys and archival materials (see Appendix E).

Purchasing media networks (cable television, radio, and newspaper). While an individual denomination may make such a purchase, the purchasing power of a large cross-denominational group is greater and more advantageous for garnering economic and media power.

Coordinating missions travel opportunities to places in the African diaspora for local church groups involved in coordinated activities (see Appendix D).

Working with African American artists (actors, visual artists, musicians, poets, and writers) in the development of a coordinated arts program that works through local churches and their surrounding communities. Such activities provide vital support for the arts, create avenues for innovation, and facilitate community fundraising potential.

calendar

Among the standard demographic topics likely to be gathered by researchers, recommended research topics to be provided in an annual State of the Faith publication with a dedicated time line are:

- numbers of African American female pastors by denomination, region of the country, and educational level;
- challenges to African American female pastors by denomination;
- number of second-career African American pastors, male and female, by denomination, region of the country, and educational level;
- percentage and value of land owned by black churches;
- number of African American churches migrating from urban to suburban settings and an explanation of the reasons for the moves;
- numbers of nondenominational churches in the country; and
- a flexible research agenda to encourage the growth of the African American faithful and the church.

appendix D
suggested coordinated diasporic activities

AS A CONTINUED EFFORT TO GET TO AMEN ON AN INTERNATIONAL level, moving into a future secured through our hands with God's blessings, the following diasporic activities provide a set of international missions activities in which local churches can become actively engaged as a group. Some local churches have active schedules of travel to places in the African diaspora and can be used as coordinating travel resources by the church community. Additionally, each denomination has its own mission and travel activities, which may additionally be aided by the national foundation (see Appendix C) to familiarize members of local churches with sites in the African diaspora through travel to specific recommended destinations on a rotational schedule. This travel is recommended to assist members of African American local congregations who have not had travel opportunities (as well as those who have) to more easily save funds for and travel to the places in which their church missions put faith into action.

calendar

Recommended below is a biennial diasporic regional twenty-five-year travel calendar that covers most places important to our historic and faith journeys. While no one in any church is expected to take all trips, seeing the entire calendar facilitates planning by the national foundation, the multidenominational church boards, and individual churches that may wish to work together, as well as individual persons who need to save funds or work with their churches on fundraising efforts to send groups on special trips.

TRIP NUMBER	YEAR	TRAVEL SITE
1	1	West Africa
2	3	Jamaica
3	5	Dominican Republic
4	7	Salvadore de Bahia, Brazil
5	9	Haiti
6	11	Holy Land
7	13	East Africa
8	15	South Africa
9	17	Windward Islands and Barbados
10	19	Egypt
11	21	Trinidad and Tobago
12	23	North Africa
13	25	Leeward Islands (Antigua and Barbuda)
Total	25 Years of Travel	

coordinated arts and travel calendar

A twenty-five-year calendar of recommended arts events (theater, dance, symphony, etc.) follows. The first few years of events are noted on the calendar. It is suggested that every fifth year the national foundation provide for the group of seminal cities (the cities for which can change each year) a list of international groups from a specific site in the diaspora that can come to the selected communities and share their particular art. In this manner, the diaspora is brought to church members unable to engage in a mission's related travel. Interspersed in the calendar are also years for local arts groups to present their talent to the community. The calendar simply makes suggestions, of course; spaces left empty allow the national foundation or the local multi-denominational church boards to find theater, symphony, or dance events that work for their communities and that showcase available, exemplary local talent in African American productions or other productions that feature us as central, pivotal characters.

YEAR	PRODUCTION
1	Maafa[1]
2	Cry
3	Lincoln Suite
4	Quincy Jones's Messiah
5	Invite Afro Caribbean group
6	Once Upon This Island
7	Local arts group
8	Langston Hughes's Black Nativity
9	
10	Brazilian group / North African Group
11	Gospel concert with symphony
12	
13	
14	Local arts group
15	West African group
16	
17	
18	
19	
20	South African group
21	Local arts group
22	
23	
24	
25	East African group

appendix E
recommended resources

african american christian resources helpful to conflict management

Hicks, Henry Beecher, Jr. *Preaching through a Storm: Confirming the Power of Preaching in the Tempest of Church Conflict.* Grand Rapids, MI: Zondervan, 1985. Describing problems that arose during a building project, "the arresting message of this book is that it is often through the preaching itself that God speaks to the issues of conflict. It is through preaching that the issues are resolved, and neither the pastor nor the people are left unchanged."

Hicks, H. Beecher. *On Jordan's Stormy Banks: Leading Your Congregation through the Wilderness of Change.* Grand Rapids, MI: Zondervan, 2004. Details how Hicks confronted the conflict in his church and community when he needed to move the church to a larger facility.

Holy Bible: The African American Jubilee Edition, King James Version. New York: American Bible Society, 1999. With historical to current resources, the Jubilee Edition is designed to "bridge the teachings of the Bible with the realities of African American day to day living."

Massey, Floyd and Samuel B. McKinney. *Church Administration in the Black Perspective.* Valley Forge, PA: Judson Press, 2003. A classic resource for understanding, organizing, and managing the church within a cultural context that can, if done well, minimize conflict.

Roberts, Deotis. *Africentric Christianity: A Theological Appraisal for Ministry.* Valley Forge, PA: Judson Press, 2000. Roberts examines the compatibility of Africentrism and Christianity and the implication of that relationship for the African American church.

Usry, Glenn, and Craig S. Keener. *Black Man's Religion.* Downer's Grove, IL: InterVarsity Press, 1996. Historians, theologians, and sociologists, these writers correct myths regarding the establishment of Christianity in Africa, its relationship to other faiths, and the documented geographical spread of the faith throughout Africa and Europe.

Wright, Jeremiah A., Jr. *Africans Who Shaped Our Faith: A Study of Ten Biblical Personalities.* Chicago, IL: Urban Ministries, 1995. Sermons about biblical Africans are accompanied by an in-depth history of each person in sociopolitical context.

archival resources

National Visionary Leadership Project. It is important for each church to have an archive that notes its history. Many church websites are now beginning this process to preserve their histories. Archives should, however, be in several forms, including online and paper, so that members and others who seek information can learn about church and pastoral history. National Visionary Leadership Project can provide churches with templates for designing archives and collecting stories that will save the important memories of their communities. http://www.visionaryproject.com/aboutusT1/aboutus.html.

Shoah Visual History Foundation. Viewing our elders and the witnesses to our history as teachers, this project was started by Steven Spielberg to capture stories of Holocaust survivors, catalogue them, and provide them in multimedia form for educational purposes to schools. His model is an instructive tool for how individual churches may wish to collect data, or how the recommended cross-denominational national foundation may wish to develop its programs. P.O. Box 3168, Los Angeles, CA 90078; http://www.vhf.org/vhfmain-2.htm.

christian conflict management

Everist, Norma Cook. *Church Conflict: From Contention to Collaboration.* Nashville: Abindgon Press, 2004. This book discusses

patterns of conflict that occur in churches, asking pastors and parishioners to begin by looking at their personal baggage, then at their
responses to conflict as it occurs. It provides useful and practical tools
for confronting conflict, seeing how to utilize the positive, defuse the
negative, and grow from both.

Howe, Leroy. *Angry People in the Pews: Managing Anger in the
Church.* Valley Forge, PA: Judson Press, 2001. This book is an excellent resource for pastors, providing them with information about why
people in their congregations may be angry and, through the use of case
studies, how those angers may best be managed in a Christian manner.

Leadership: Real Ministry in a Complex World 25, no. 4 (Fall
2004). The entire issue deals with conflict, from articles provided by
pastors, lay leaders, and outside experts to surveys and the results of
panel discussions.

McKinney, Lora-Ellen. *View from the Pew: What Preachers Can
Learn from Church Members.* Valley Forge, PA: Judson Press, 2003.
A book of recommendations from the pew to the pulpit on how to
organize worship for excellence; a primary focus of the recommendations is on loving communication with the pew.

conflict management

The Alban Institute. Since its inception, the Alban Institute has earned
a reputation as a leader in addressing congregational conflict management issues through its research, consulting services, educational
events, and particularly its publications. 2121 Cooperative Way, Suite
100, Herndon, VA 20171; 703-964-2700 (phone), 800-486-1318
(phone); 703-964-0370 (fax); www.alban.org.

Association for Conflict Resolution. The Association for Conflict
Resolution (ACR) is a professional organization dedicated to enhancing the practice and public understanding of conflict resolution. Serving
a diverse national and international audience that includes more than
6,000 mediators, arbitrators, facilitators, and educators, ACR has local
offices in most major cities and can provide conflict resolution services

to churches in their areas. They can also be utilized as trainers for local churches and church councils who wish to learn effective mediation strategies for conflict resolution and collaborative decisionmaking. Association for Conflict Resolution, 1015 18th Street, NW, Suite 1150, Washington, DC 20036; 202-464-9700 (phone); 202-464-9720 (fax); acr@ACRnet.org.

Fisher, Roger, and Scott Brown. *Getting Together: Building Relationships as We Negotiate*. New York: Penguin Books, 1988. A complement to *Getting to Yes*, this book adds additional steps to the negotiation and relationship-building process.

Fisher, Roger; William Ury; and Bruce Patton. *Getting to Yes: Negotiating Agreement Without Giving In*. New York: Penguin Books, 1991. This negotiation classic has been translated into eighteen languages and has sold over 1 million copies since it was originally published in 1981.

Peacemaker Ministries. Peacemaker Ministries provides comprehensive domestic and international training to multicultural audiences on Cultivating the Culture of Peace, a multi-level approach to change churches from cultures of disbelief in which people lack practical training in resolving conflict and doubt that the church can do much to help them resolve their differences, to cultures of multiplication, in which people delight in expanding God's kingdom by showing other people and churches how they too can be peacemakers. Training includes a focus on the characteristics of peace (vision, training, assistance, perseverance, accountability, restoration, and witness). P.O. Box 81130, Billings, MT 59108; 406-256-1583; www.Peace-maker.net.

Ury, William. *Getting Past No: Negotiating Your Way from Confrontation to Cooperation*. New York: Bantam, revised edition 1993. William Ury builds on the principals put forth in his first book with Roger Fisher, *Getting to Yes*. In *Getting Past No*, Ury discusses the nuances and niceties of negotiating using a joint problem-solving approach that is "interest based" rather than being "rights based" or "power based." Ury explains that the challenge is to convert a confrontational situation to a cooperative creative problem.

ethics

Grace, Bill. *Ethical Leadership: In Pursuit of the Common Good.* Seattle, WA: Center for Ethical Leadership, 1999. Ethical leaders do not exist for themselves, but are called to lead for the common good. The book forwards principles about justice, care, and compassion.

Roberts, Samuel K. *African American Christian Ethics.* Cleveland, OH: The Pilgrim Press, 2001. Roberts builds an ethic upon a Trinitarian foundation and explores scripture, tradition, human experience, and reason as sources for such an ethic. Using this framework, he examines critical issues, including human sexuality and family life, medicine and bioethics, and pursuit of justice.

HIV/AIDS

Balm in Gilead. Founded in 1989, this organization provides HIV/AIDS education for African American churches, taking its name from Jeremiah 8:22, which refers to healing during times of illness. The motto is, "Our people, our problem, our solution." 130 W. 42nd Street, #450, New York, NY 10036; 888-225-6243; www.balmingilead.org.

Lott Carey—See International Missions section.

international missions

Lott Carey. The Lott Carey Foreign Mission Convention focuses on ministry, health, and education. They provide an international HIV/AIDS Initiative in collaboration with indigenous faith communities, government agencies, and nongovernmental organizations; assist health care organizations and workers; run a pastoral excellence program to stimulate peer-based theological reflection and networking opportunities; and maintain programs to alleviate poverty and empower women. 220 I (Eye) Street NE, Suite 220, Washington DC, 20002-4389; 202-543-3200 (phone); 202-543-6300 (fax); www.lottcarey.org.

pastoral care

June, Lee N., and Sabrina D. Black (editors). *Counseling in African-American Communities: Biblical Perspectives on Tough Issues.* Grand Rapids, MI: Zondervan, 2002. Offering a biblically based guide for those who counsel African Americans, this book by African Americans addresses such issues as mental illness, addiction, grief, divorce, and domestic violence.

Shawchuck, Norman, and Roger Heuser. *Leading the Congregation: Caring for Yourself While Serving the People.* Nashville, TN: Abingdon, 1993. This book provides targeted strategies by which pastors can assess their needs, understanding that well-tended, honest, and focused shepherds are better leaders for their Christian flocks.

Wimberly, Edward P. *Relational Refugees: Alienation and Reincorporation in African American Churches and Communities.* Nashville, TN: Abingdon Press, 2000. Using the premise that our society increasingly produces people who are disconnected from one another (relational refugees), this book presents a model of pastoral care that, through mentoring relationships important to African Americans and notable in the lives of preachers, help people reconnect to society through the tools of the church.

practical and spiritual

George, Elizabeth. *A Woman's Walk with God: Growing in the Fruit of the Spirit.* Eugene, OR: Harvest House, 1995. Heralded as a spiritual teacher whose books change women's lives, George addresses in this book attitudes, actions, and applications of the fruit of the Spirit.

Heifitz, Ronald A. *Leadership without Easy Answers.* Cambridge, MA: The Belknap Press of Harvard University Press, 1994. A professor at the Kennedy School of Government at Harvard University with a reputation for innovative, practical, and easy-to-implement theories, Dr. Heifitz, a psychiatrist and skilled musician, pushes leaders to think strategically about how to engage action from positions of authority.

Hirsch, Peter. *Success by Design: Ten Biblical Secrets to Help You*

Achieve Your God-Given Potential. Minneapolis, MN: Bethany House, 2002. Hirsch, a devout Jew, met Christ and arrived at God's blueprint for successful living.

Zander, Rosamund Stone, and Benjamin Zander. *The Art of Possibility.* Cambridge, MA: Harvard Business School Press, 2000. This couple, a psychotherapist-painter and her husband, the director of the Boston Philharmonic, provide an innovative collection of practices designed to change our outlook for dealing with life's challenges, personally and interpersonally. Through the language of art, they open up new worlds of personal potential and, as a result, new realms of possibility.

research and survey assistance

The National Congregations Study (NCS) was conducted in conjunction with the 1998 General Social Survey (GSS). The tools on this website, used for this study, can be used by local community churches as is or can be adapted to learn about the religious habits and patterns in your community. From the Alban Institute site, access the NCS link. http://www.alban.org/NatCongStudy.asp.

study guides

African American Heritage Hymnal. Though most African American churches are not theological liturgical, it is helpful to have guidelines by which to structure important moments in our year. In addition to cataloguing the songs of our foreparents, Wesleyan hymns, and new classics, the hymnal provides for the first time an African American liturgical year and responsive readings that incorporate our heroes. Additionally, the book is edited by and many of its songs are arranged by African American musicians. Published by GIA Publications, Chicago, 2001.

Women of Color Study Bible (KJV). This Bible was created by and for contemporary women of African American descent. The commentaries and reference materials in the *Women of Color Study Bible* include the life lessons, skills, and interpretations of 120 writers, female clergy, editors, and contributors. Prior to each book of the Bible, readers will find an Afrocentric design as well as a synopsis that provides historical information and notable black personalities in that book.

websites—african american–centered christianity

www.blackandchristian.com. Dedicated to the provision of support to African American churches, this site provides clergy and leadership resources (The Pulpit); family ministry and African American website links (The Pew); theological resources for scholars, educators, and students (The Academy); historical and reference material on the African American church (The Black Church); and links to Africa and the diaspora (BNC Global).

www.everythingblack.com. This site contains links to a variety of black websites (keyword: religion).

www.monastereo.com. This site bills itself as a comprehensive black Christian search tool.

websites—christianity

The Alban Institute (www.alban.org). This website provides research on mainline Protestant denominations and an African American leadership institute.

Barna Research Online (www.barna.org). This website provides statistics on religion and religious practice in the United States, offering comparisons between racial and ethnic groups.

websites—health and history

www.dvinstitute.org. The Institute on Domestic Violence in the African American Community provides leadership in the effort to reduce/end violence through a bibliography, hotline numbers, events, and a newsletter.

www.pbs.org/gointochicago/resources/biblio2.html. This list of books, films, and websites on black migration from the North to the South was compiled for a PBS series entitled *Goin' to Chicago*.

www.ResolveChurchConflict.com. This national service, begun by Ken Newberger, Ph.D., urges churches to "learn to move forward in a manner that honors God, improves ministry and restores relationships." A four-page document on resolving church conflict can be obtained by calling 301-253-8877.

websites of african american denominations

African Methodist Episcopal (AME) Church—www.amecnet.org

African Methodist Episcopal Zion (AMEZ) Church—www.theamezionchurch.org

Christian Methodist Episcopal (CME) Church—www.c-m-e.org

National Baptist Convention, USA, Incorporated (NBC)—www.nbc-usa.org

National Baptist Convention of America (NBCA)—www.nbcamerica.com

National Missionary Baptist Convention of America (NMBCA)—www.nmbca.com

Progressive National Baptist Convention (PNBC)—www.pnbc.org

Church of God in Christ (COGIC)—www.cogic.org

INTRODUCTION

1. "Been in the Storm So Long," nineteenth-century Negro spiritual. This song was selected to begin *Getting to Amen* because so many of us have grown so accustomed to behaving in particular ways that we simply cannot easily change. Behaviors that are habitual require, at a minimum, prayer, and an acknowledgment that having been in the storm does not require one to stay in the storm. Storms, after all, are always followed by calm.

2. How else might we explain the absolute importance that we give to fights over the color and style of choir robes or the political infighting over who will become the next chair of the board of trustees? The ways in which these decisions get made often go far beyond any spiritual goal of building the church in Christ's name.

3. Roger Fisher, William Ury, and Bruce Patton, *Getting to Yes: Negotiating Agreement without Giving In* (New York: Penguin Books, 1991), 3.

4. Ibid., 17.

5. Ibid., 40.

6. Ibid., 56.

7. Ibid., 80.

CHAPTER 1: WHAT THE TRIBE NEEDS TO KNOW

1. www.barna.org, accessed on October 8, 2004.

2. For a caveman, for example, protecting one's territory kept one safe from predators who were likely to steal food that was essential for life. Protecting territory successfully for an extended period of time gave one an established or perceived prominence in an area and resulted in a thriving community.

3. War is an odd enterprise. Among industrialized countries such as ours who follow the rule of law, war occurs through written agreements, ends for brief moment by ceasefires, and may even have predetermined battle lines. Such organized warfare can differ from tribal wars, though both may have genocide, a terrible end, as a goal.

4. Goodwin Watson and David Johnson, *Social Psychology: Issues and Insights,* 2nd ed. (New York: J. B. Lippincott: 1972), 375–76.

5. The respect that women are accorded in the church is tempered. It is often limited to honorific titles, while roles of authentic power such as pastor or deacon are not typically available to them. While there are several notable exceptions to this—Rev. Vashti McKenzie is the first female AME bishop (2000) and Barbara Harris is the first female Anglican bishop (1998), and autonomous Baptist churches can decide for themselves if they will ordain female deacons—most women do their work in Sunday

school, on missions societies, and in other traditional capacities of "women's" work, even though they comprise the majority of the congregation and of the tithers on any given Sunday morning.

6. Something as simple as making a list entitled "What I Like About You" and sharing it is a great conflict management tool.

7. Elliott Aronson, *The Social Animal* (San Francisco: W. H. Freeman and Company, 1972), 238.

8. Norma Cook Everist, *Church Conflict: From Contention to Collaboration* (Nashville: Abindgon Press, 2004), 28–29.

9. Freud named the three portions of the personality the id (primitive, primary, sexualized and uninhibited portion), the ego (the realistic portion of the personality that adapts and changes), and the superego (the parental personality that monitors morality).

10. Freud, of Jewish ancestry, was beginning his theories in Austria, during the years preceding WWII. He was quite interested in how people identified themselves as members of groups or societies. Freud's theory was that groups turn over to leaders the moral-setting role of parent (superego), which can produce the very dangerous kind of lock-step thinking that occurred in Hitler's Germany. In this extreme case, those who fought against rules were met with death. In churches and other settings, lock-step thinking can lead to other forms of groupthink, in which no one is willing to challenge a leader and no creative thinking occurs.

11. John Paul Lederach, *Preparing for Peace: Conflict Transformation across Cultures* (Syracuse, NY: Syracuse University Press, 1995), 22.

12. Bruce Weinstein, *What Should I Do? 4 Simple Steps to Making Better Decisions in Everyday Life* (New York: Perigee Books, 2000), 16.

13. Watson and Johnson, *Social Psychology*, 387.

14. The average church in the United States has a single pastor and a median number of 250 members. www.barna.org, accessed on October 8, 2004.

15. This is the modern version of how people fight to establish territoriality.

16. How appointed positions occur are denominationally dependent.

17. The positions of status are important and are to be taken seriously. However, we tend to take them so seriously that we think that we are more important than those who have not been given similar titles. The titles are artificial to the degree that they do not designate our personal importance; rather, they simply indicate the task that we have been asked to do for Christ. In many cases, these are, of course, tasks we can do whether or not we have been given a specific title.

18. In the Trinity United Church of Christ, congregants are encouraged to think strategically about how they use language to empower themselves. They are asked not to use the language of the oppressor to put down one another. The N-word and terms that specify social class distinctions are examples of disempowering language.

19. For example, our contributions to science, classical music, philosophy, and other realms considered to be intellectually rigorous are less likely to be acknowledged.

20. A human skull found in Chad (central Africa) is reported to be the oldest human archeological remains (6–7 million years old), leading to new beliefs about the origin

of man. www.google.com (keywords: ancient skull Chad) and www.cnn.com /2002/TECH/science/07/10/ancient.skull, accessed on October 12, 2004.

21. To those likely to believe genetic racial theories, our apparent inability to govern ourselves when colonial powers retreated from African nations provides "proof" of our "inherent inequality."

22. Joel Kotkin, *Tribes: How Race, Religion and Identity Determine Success in the New Global Economy* (New York: Random House, 1994), 36–68.

23. It is part of what makes for some of our best comedy and drama. Games like "the dozens" are part of our positive interpersonal cultural combativeness—they are linguistic fun, a street precursor to the poetry slams and Russell Simmon's Def Poetry Jam. The standup comedy of these new forms, as diverse as Moms Mabley, Bill Cosby, Richard Pryor, Eddie Murphy, Chris Rock, and the Pulitzer Prize–winning multigenerational drama of August Wilson, have all drawn on that same interpersonal linguistic combativeness to demonstrate how humor, ingenuity, and love have contributed to our survival strategies in a difficult world.

24. African Americans, for example, are much more likely than other ethnic and racial groups to engage in informal adoptions, raising other people's children as our own.

25. It continues to be popular to blame "the man," when, though "the man" or the system represented by "him" may be the continued root of our problems, we must be responsible for our personal choices. We were also aided by American cultural factors. The 1980s was the era of the victim, one in which we learned to name our disorders and actively claim and embrace our pathologies. While there is a usefulness and empowerment to the process of naming, it is ultimately more empowering to claim change for oneself.

26. www.barna.org, accessed on November 19, 2004.

CHAPTER 2: AFRICAN AMERICAN CHRISTIAN ETHICS

1. A more detailed history of the National Baptists can be found in C. Eric Lincoln and Lawrence H. Mamiya's *The Black Church in the African American Experience* (Durham, N.C.: Duke University Press, 1990), 22–30.

2. Leonard Pitts. "Tired Men Don't Care What White People Think." *Seattle Times*, July 11, 2004.

3. Ibid.

4. Human Rights Watch state by state statistics, http://www.hrw.org /backgrounder/usa/incarceration/, accessed on December 28, 2004.

5. Pitts, "Tired Men." Ibid.

6. Craig S. Keener and Glenn Usry, *Defending Black Faith: Answers to Tough Questions about African American Christianity* (Downers Grove, IL, InterVarsity Press, 1997), 14.

7. Samuel K. Roberts, *African American Christian Ethics* (Cleveland, OH, Pilgrim Press, 2001), 45.

8. Henry and Ella Mitchell, in a letter to the author dated April 26, 2002, reprinted

in Lora-Ellen McKinney, *Total Praise! An Orientation to Baptist Belief and Worship* (Valley Forge, PA.: Judson Press, 2003), 52–53.

9. *Encarta Dictionary*, 2003. Keyword: ethics.

10. Henry H. Mitchell and Nicholas Cooper Lewter, *Soul Theology: The Heart of American Black Culture* (San Francisco: Harper and Row, 1986), 3.

11. Roberts, *African American Christian Ethics*, 125.

12. Written by a number of authors, the information in the Old Testament is presented in sections that describe law, history, poetry and wisdom, and the major and minor prophets. It further describes the faith and religious life of the people of Israel. Written by followers of Jesus Christ, the New Testament provides the Gospels, Paul's letters, history, prophecy, and general letters so that "good news" can be spread and new life in Christ can be available to them.

13. An excellent discussion of African lands in the Bible can be found in the *African American Heritage Study Bible*. See Appendix E.

14. From "No Greater Love."

15. People of European descent hold power, though people of color are more numerous in the world.

16. The image of a black Christ was painted by Vermont artist Janet McKenzie. It can be viewed at www.africana.com, www.natcath.com, or located by www.google.com (keywords: Catholic Reporter Black Jesus), accessed on November 27, 2004.

17. Thurgood Marshall Documentary, See 10:00 a.m., November 26, 2004. www.kuow.org/weekday.asp?Archive=11-26, accessed on November 27, 2004.

18. "Ride on, King Jesus," *African American Heritage Hymnal* (Chicago: GIA Publications, Inc., 2001), no. 225.

19. The most known of the slave rebellions was the Nat Turner Rebellion. Born into slavery, Nat Turner inherited a deep hatred of slavery from his mother and grandmother. Able to read and write, he received a vision from God to rise up against slavery. On August 21, 1831, he and 7 other slaves killed his master, were joined by 75 more slaves, and killed 60 more whites. Three-thousand state militia ended the uprising, killing 100 slaves not involved in the fighting. Nat Turner was executed on November 11, 1831.

20. It must also be noted that this same model of democracy is what many scholars believe has created such anger in many in the Muslim world, including those who engaged in the September 11, 2001, attacks on the United States. Those attacks were the result of a misinterpretation of the reading of the Koran based on an anger over economic disparities between our countries and a perception of U.S. policies that favor Israel over Palestine.

21. Among other things, cemeteries teach the relative social positions of men and women, of racial and ethnic groups, of children in relation to their parents and in society in general. For example, in the early 1900s, many wives were buried next to their husbands with only the label "wife" and no name. Until the Civil Rights Act was passed, cemeteries segregated the races and separated Jews and Christians for burial as well. Additionally, until the 1900s, social class was clear on tombstones through various markings on the tomb stonework as well as their size. Wealthy families buried their dead in

mausoleums in which they could segregate their family members within an otherwise open cemetery, sometimes also creating a lake or other beautiful setting. Middle-class families showed their status by noting their type of work on the tomb: for example, farm families had wheat sheaves on their tombs. Soldiers were noted by military swords and hats, positioned to demonstrate that they had served honorably or had been killed in battle. This kind of structure to cemeteries was, for me, a very interesting way of learning about the ways that societies were organized and individual families valued one another.

22. Liberty as personal choice is not being discussed as the difference between the theologies of predestination and free will. Instead, it is meant only to indicate that liberty, the opportunity to live as a person free from sin, is an option that we can make.

23. "There Is a Balm in Gilead," *African American Heritage Hymnal* (Chicago: GIA Publications, Inc., 2001), no. 524.

24. Roberts, *African American Christian Ethics*, 100.

25. http://www.thewords.com/l-palau/definitions/spirit.htm, accessed on November 29, 2004.

26. Roberts, *African American Christian Ethics*, 99.

27. Depending upon the particular tenets of our faiths, the ages of our baptisms may differ, as will, then, our awareness of the Holy Spirit in our lives. For example, those baptized as infants will, like AME members, of necessity, not become aware of the Holy Spirit, though he is there, until later in their lives, while Baptists cannot become baptized until they have a conscious awareness of Christ.

28. Testimony of a former slave, "God Struck Me Dead," as recorded in Roberts, *African American Christian Ethics*, 99.

29. http://www.cathygoddard.com/song4.php, accessed on November 28, 2004.

30. "Amazing Grace," text by John Newton, tune (Virginia Harmony) arranged by Evelyn Simpson-Curenton, *African American Heritage Hymnal* (Chicago: GIA Publications, Inc., 2001), no. 271.

31. http://www.gsu.edu/~wwwcou/lifeshops/conflictpsy.htm, accessed on October 22, 2004.

32. Firefighters, police officers, and emergency medical staff are generally classified as first responders.

CHAPTER 3: ANGER IN PERSPECTIVE

1. Leroy Howe, *Angry People in the Pews: Managing Anger in the Church* (Valley Forge, PA.: Judson Press, 2001), 32.

2. Kenneth C. Haugk, *Antagonists in the Church: How to Identify and Deal with Destructive Conflict* (Minneapolis: Augsburg Publishing House, 1988), 26.

3. Ibid. Nonsubstantive evidence has little basis in fact; insatiable demands indicate that antagonists are never satisfied.

4. Ibid., 26–29.

5. Howe, *Angry People in the Pews*, 2.

6. The Nick at Night cable station has become increasingly popular. Additionally, a

recent *60 Minutes* reported that *The Lawrence Welk Show*, a Sunday night variety show from the 1950s and 1960s, has become the most popular show on cable. Perhaps because it harkens back to a safer, calmer time. Given its reported popularity, its watchers are not just older persons who want trips down memory lane.

7. www.barna.org, 1998 report, 19.

8. Ibid.

CHAPTER 4: PRINCIPLES AND PERSPECTIVES
FOR MANAGING CONFLICT

1. Barack Obama, usatoday.com, www.usatoday.com/news/politicselections/nation/president/2004-07-27-obama-speech-text_x.htm?POE=click-refer, accessed on November 19, 2004.

2. Not an educated woman, Laura Lee Stewart Jones (1913–1998) was perhaps the smartest person I have known, because her mother-wit always helped her figure out the most important truths.

3. Marshall Shelley, "Resolutely Redemptive," *Leadership: Real Ministry in a Complex World 25, no. 4* (Fall 2004): 3.

4. This concept of being "a person from their own coasts" is forwarded by Rev. Dr. Gardner C. Taylor, senior pastor emeritus of Concord Baptist Church of Christ in Brooklyn, New York. Dr. Taylor is widely regarded as a preeminent teacher-mentor to preachers.

5. Lora-Ellen McKinney, *View from the Pew: What Preachers Can Learn from Church Members* (Valley Forge, PA.: Judson Press: 2004), 28.

6. Lawrence H. Summers, "John Harvard's Journal," *Harvard Magazine* (July–August 2004): 50.

7. Floyd Massey Jr. and Samuel Berry McKinney, *Church Administration in the Black Perspective* (Valley Forge, PA.: Judson Press, 1976, revised 2003), 41.

8. Ibid., 51–52.

9. Cooley, "Ghosts of Conflicts Past," *Leadership: Real Ministry in a Complex World* 25, no. 4 (Fall 2004): 37.

10. "Leadership Surveys Church Conflict," *Leadership: Real Ministry in a Complex World* 25, no. 4 (Fall 2004): 25.

11. Cooley, "Ghosts of Conflicts Past," 37.

12. Rene Schlaepfer, "Keeping Conflict Healthy, The Leadership Forum," *Leadership: Real Ministry in a Complex World*, 25, no. 4 (Fall 2004): 21.

CHAPTER 5: THE 8 P'S: 8 STRATEGIES
FOR MANAGING CONFLICT

1. Adapted. Earlier lyrics can be found in *The Trouble I've Seen: the big book of NEGRO SPIRITUALS* (Valley Forge, Pa.: Judson Press, 2003), 135.

2. John Paul Lederach's site: http://www.emu.edu/humanresources/personnel/pages
/lederacj.html, accessed on December 4, 2004. A speech to the Community Relations
Council on Sustainability http://www.community-relations.org.uk/about_the_coun-
cil/background_info/john_paul_lederach_speech/, accessed on December 4, 2004.

3. This is a detailed and accurate account of the election in El Salvador, accessed on
December 4, 2004: http://zena.secureforum.com/Znet/zmag/articles/petrasjuly
97.html. Another interesting article on the history of the country can be found at
http://www.abacci.com/atlas/history.asp?countryID=188, accessed December 4,
2004.

4. Bruce Weinstein, *What Should I Do? 4 Simple Steps to Making Better Decisions in
Everyday Life* (New York: Perigee Books, 2000). The steps are Dr. Weinstein's; the
examples are the author's.

5. It may seem odd to some to separate personal values from Christian values. They
will, in most cases, be the same. A personal value may be, for example, that one will
never, for the sake of personal health, involve oneself in situations where people
scream at one another, as this may raise blood pressure, create psychological depression, and depress the immune system. Life is short, after all, and research has recently demonstrated that life is shortened by certain stressors such as the one mentioned
in this example. While the Christian value tells us to treat each other well, a value that
should facilitate long life, the personal idiosyncrasies that might attend a personal
value can cause individuals to view it as a separate category. Another more obvious
example is that while our Christian values may tell us that premarital sex is wrong,
many people allow their personal values to engage in the behavior nonetheless.

6. http://www.rottentomatoes.com/m/ran/about.php, accessed on December 1, 2004.
This is a searchable movie review database. If the review is not automatically accessi-
ble, enter the movie name (Ran) and the director's name (Akira Kurosawa) to read
the review.

7. Norma Cook Everist, *Church Conflict: From Contention to Collaboration*
(Nashville: Abindgon Press, 2004). In Norma Everist's version, they are not referred
to as ABC's, and "bartering" is known as "collaboration." Neither was
"Compassion" one of Ms. Everist's original categories. In the text, the categories are
Ms. Everist's, except as noted; the examples are the author's.

8. While among Americans, many African Americans understood the terrorist attacks
differently than the general population, given our initial involuntary American status
as slaves and our later experiences, in our own country, of being under legislative and
personal attack. Nonetheless, on that day we had an American identity.

9. Norma Cook Everist, *Church Conflict: From Contention to Collaboration*
(Nashville: Abindgon Press, 2004), 146.

10. "The Road Not Taken" is part of a larger piece by Robert Frost entitled
"Mountain Interlude," http://www.bartleby.com/119/1.html, accessed on December
1, 2004.

CHAPTER 6: WOMEN IN CHURCH LEADERSHIP

1. Beth Wolk, "Women and the Church—North America," *Religious Traditions of the African Diaspora*," http://dickinsg.intrasun.tcnj.edu/diaspora/women.html, accessed on December 21, 2004.

2. Ibid.

3. First ladies of the church have often seen their roles in two ways: the traditional manner in which they were subservient to their husbands and served the church by becoming responsible to one of its stereotypically female ministries, or by being the power behind the pulpit, acting in an unofficial advisory role to their husbands. Increasingly, especially in COGIC and nondenominational churches, first ladies have visible roles in partnership with their husbands, frequently as co-pastors with or without formal ordination.

4. Wolk, "Women in the Church."

5. Ibid.

6. "Women Are the Backbone of the Christian Congregations in America," March 6, 2000, www.barna.org.

7. "Phillis [Wheatley] became a Boston sensation after she wrote a poem on the death of the evangelical preacher George Whitefield in 1770. Three years later thirty-nine of her poems were published in London as *Poems on Various Subjects, Religious and Moral*. It was the first book to be published by a black American." http://earlyamerica.com/review/winter96/wheatley.html, accessed on December 7, 2004.

8. Elizabeth George, *A Woman's Walk with God: Growing in the Fruit of the Spirit* (Eugene, OR: Harvest House, 2000), 116–17.

9. Peter Gomes, "Anne Hutchinson: Brief Life of Harvard's 'Midwife': 1595–1643," *Harvard Magazine* (November–December 2002): 32.

10. Ibid.

11. This interpretation of Scripture believes that there is historical, chronological, social context and that the Bible was written by different authors at different points in time who were inspired by God.

12. Henry Beecher Hicks Jr., "A Rationale for Female Deacons," lecture given at Metropolitan Baptist Church, Washington, DC, in 1991.

13. Readers, though the world is changing, please excuse the stereotype. The power differential is such that this is a likely scenario, so, for ease of writing, the male dominant scenario is an assumption that I am making.

14. H. B. London Jr. and Neil B. Wiseman, *The Heart of a Great Pastor: How to Grow Strong and Thrive Where God Has Planted You* (Ventura, CA: Regal Books, 1994), 73.

15. Maya Angelou, Life Mosaic greeting card, © 2003 Hallmark Cards.

CHAPTER 7: HOMOSEXUALITY

1. "An Evening Prayer," words and music by C. Maude Battersby, arranged by Charles H. Gabriel circa 1911. The Musical Instrument Digital Interface is available

so that this song can be played at http://www.cyberhymnal.org/htm/e/v/evprayer.htm.
2. Deborah Shmueli, Conflict Assessment, www.beyondintractability.org/m/conflict_
assessment.jsp, accessed on December 8, 2004.
3. Ibid. The author made adaptations to the process so that it would work more
smoothly in a church setting.

CHAPTER 8: CHURCH MIGRATION
1. It is essential that all of our musical traditions, from spirituals through hip-hop
gospel, be part of our services.
2. This definition of megachurch goes beyond the number and size definition to
describe pastoral charismatic oversight, theological approach typically outside of an
established denomination, familial management and often actual ownership of
church building, land and holdings, and evangelical outreach focused primarily on
new, rather than established Christians.
3. Some changes are noted not to be enhancements, but are architectural alterations
that destroy historic facades, replacing them, rather than incorporating the old with
the new.
4. Wendell Griffen, "The Crisis Facing Black Christians in the 21st Century," deliv-
ered during the E. C. Morris Ministers Institute, Arkansas Baptist College, Little
Rock, Arkansas, April 5–7, 2005.
5. "The Church's One Foundation," lyrics by The Reverend Pamela June Anderson,
D. Min. in *African American Heritage Hymnal*, (Chicago: GIA Publications, 2001),
337. Used by permission.
6. Rosamund Stone Zander and Benjamin Zander, *The Art of Possibility* (Cambridge:
Harvard Business School Press, 2000), 73. Church reference in parentheses is the
author's.
7. Mark Buchanan, "The Good Fight: Four Spiritual Disciplines to Keep Fights from
Scarring Your Soul," *Leadership: Real Ministry in a Complex World* 25, no. 4 (Fall
2004): 52.
8. Ibid., 55.
9. Ibid., 56.
10. The National Visionary Leadership Project, www.visionaryproject.com
/aboutusT1/aboutus.html, accessed on April 17, 2005.
11. The Survivors of the Shoah Visual History Foundation, http://www.vhf.org/vhf-
main-2.htm, accessed on December 30, 2004.
12. H. Beecher Hicks Jr., *On Jordan's Stormy Banks: Leading Your Congregation
Through the Wilderness of Change* (Grand Rapids: Zondervan, 2004), 101.
13. Peacemaker Ministries, "Transforming Your Church: Cultivating a Culture of
Peace," http://www.hispeace.org/html/church_COP.htm, accessed on April 18, 2005.

CHAPTER 9: POLITICS AND PREACHING

1. Former President William J. Clinton at the inaugural of his library, Little Rock, Arkansas, as printed in an article by Sidney Blumenthal, "Counterinaugural at the Clinton Library," www.Salon.com, accessed on November 27, 2004.

2. See www.pnbc.org (About Us/History/Call Letter). The other cause of the split was tenure of the President J. H. Jackson's office; accessed on April 17, 2005.

3. Typically, the National Missionary Baptist Convention (NMBC) is not numbered among the seven traditionally African American denominations. There are usually three Baptist conventions (NBC-USA, Inc., NBC of America, and PNBC), along with AME, AME Zion, CME, and COGIC, that are noted to comprise black denominational structures. It is not clear at the time of this book's publication if this system will be revised to include the NMBC or how the 2005 conciliatory meetings of the Baptist groups may affect the traditional organizations.

4. Aaron Counts and Larry Evans, "Be Light unto Ourselves: Black America Must Look Inward for Healing Solutions," *Seattle Times*, November 21, 2004, sec. D1.

5. Ibid.

6. Now that television cameras attend most community events, it is essential that ministers determine who will be the spokesperson for a particular issue so that no such potential embarrassments occur. Though I do not recall the specific topical event, I remember a CNN press conference where it was so clear that ministers not accustomed to the limelight were clamoring for it that they had created conflict among themselves, made their community look bad in the nation's eyes, and seemed to be temporarily less concerned with the devastating issue that had placed them in front of the cameras than their own self-aggrandizement.

7. Norman Shawchuck and and Roger Heuser, *Leading the Congregation: Caring for Yourself While Serving the People* (Nashville: Abingdon Press, 1993), 104–5. Items 1–3 are Kenneth Blanchard and Norman Vincent Peale's. Items 4–5 are Shawchuck and Heuser's.

8. Rev. Jim Wallis, convener, "Call to Renewal," statement made on *Meet the Press*, NBC TV, November 28, 2004.

9. H. Beecher Hicks Jr., *On Jordan's Stormy Banks: Leading Your Congregation through the Wilderness of Change* (Grand Rapids: Zondervan, 2004), 101.

10. James Surowiecki, *The Wisdom of Crowds: Why the Many Are Smarter Than the Few and How the Collective Wisdom Shapes Business, Economies, Societies and Nations* (New York: Doubleday, 2004), xix.

11. Bay of Pigs, http://www.globalsecurity.org/intell/ops/bay-of-pigs.htm; http://www.probe.org/docs/jfk.html, accessed on December 27, 2004.

12. Groupthink is based on a concept identified by Drs. I. L. Janis and L. Mann in 1977. The eight primary symptoms can be found on http://www.cedu.niu.edu /~fulmer/groupthink.htm, accessed on April 17, 2005.

13. www.naacp.org can provide information regarding local community resources.

14. See the NAACP's website, www.naacp.org, for more information.

15. Abraham Lincoln's second inaugural speech, http://www.classbrain.com/art-teenst/publish/article_79.shtml's, accessed on Decem-ber 26, 2004.

CHAPTER 10: NONDENOMINATIONALISM

1. E-mail conversation with Dr. H. Beecher Hicks regarding nondenominationalism on October 9, 2003.

2. While creating a place for the practice of a specific set of faith beliefs may be the reason that a pastor forms a nondenominational church, the congregations are often not likely to speak the language of dogma and theology that is part of the denominational structure. Increasingly, however, denominationally affiliated churches find that their parishioners are not uniformly conversant with the tenets of their faiths and, to address this concern, have designed new members classes in which tenets are taught.

3. T. M. Robinson, http://supremejustice.net/baptist/nondenom.html, accessed on December 20, 2004.

4. Richard Gruhn, "Nondenominational Churches Thrive," *The San Angelo Standard*, http://web.gosanangelo.com/archive/98/july/23/letters.htm, accessed on December 20, 2004.

5. Richard Allen was the founder of the AME Church.

6. Quassey was the first known black Baptist, registered in 1743 as one of fifty-one members of the Baptist church in Newton, Rhode Island.

7. Industrial Revolution, http://mars.acnet.wnec.edu/~grempel/courses/wc2/lectures/industrialrev.html, accessed on December 21, 2004.

8. Peter Smith, "Empty Pulpit: Ranks of Pastors Dwindling," *Courier Journal*, 4 April 2004, http://www.courier-journal.com/cjextra/2004projects/empty_pulpits/day1/A1-pastors0404-16834.html, accessed on December 28, 2004.

9. Ibid. In the study, it is important to note that data was available for white mainline denominations, including Pentecostal groups, though data was not reported for African American denominations.

10. Lora-Ellen McKinney, *Total Praise: An Orientation to Black Baptist Belief and Worship* (Valley Forge, PA.: Judson Press, 2003), 118.

11. It is important for each church to have an archive that notes its history. Many church websites are now beginning this process to preserve their histories. Archives should, however, be in several forms, including online, on disk, DVD, CD, and paper, so that members and others who seek information can learn about church and pastoral history. Other national resources, such as http://www.visionaryproject.com/aboutusT1/ aboutus.html can provide churches with templates for designing archives and collecting stories that will save the important memories of their communities.

12. Nondenominationalism, www.barna.org, accessed on December 20, 2004.

13. Information about Creflo Dollar can be found at www.worldchangers.org (World Changers Church International); www.creflodollarministries.org (Creflo Dollar Ministries), accessed on December 20, 2004. There is also an excellent article on the

Creflo Dollar Ministries in *The New Yorker*: Kelefa Sanneh, "Letter from Atlanta: Pray and Grow Rich (Dr. Creflo Dollar's Ministry of Money)," *The New Yorker* (October 11, 2004): 48.

14. "Prayer for the Courage to Take Risks" by Vienna Cobb Anderson, adapted from "Prayers of Our Hearts," 1991, http://www.beliefnet.com/prayeroftheday/more_prayers.asp?paid=63&faid=3, accessed on December 3, 2004.

15. Peter L. Steinke, "Healthy Congregations: A Systems Approach," http://www.alban.org/ResearchInfo.asp?ID=33, accessed on April 17, 2005.

16. Daneen Skube, *The Seattle Times and Post Intelligencer*, December 12, 2004, sec. H1.

17. Kelefa Sanneh, "Letter from Atlanta, 52. Italics are the author's, indicating that this is a very new way of thinking about the congregant as more than a soul to save.

CHAPTER 11: WHY GOD DON'T LIKE UGLY: PROPOSING A COLLABORATIVE FUTURE

1. To read the entire poem, go to www.google.com (keywords: white man's burden kipling), accessed on October 26, 2002.

2. Lawrence Little, "The African Methodist Episcopal Church Media and Racial Discourse, 1880–1900," *The North Star* 2, no. 1 (Fall 1998): 5. http://northstar.vassar.edu, accessed on October 25, 2002.

3. Ibid.

CHAPTER 12: RECLAIMING THE TRIBE: TAKING OFF THE SHACKLES IN JESUS' NAME

1. "Get Together," written by Jesse Colin Young, The Youngbloods (biography available at http://www.classicbands.com/youngbloods.html). Jesse Colin Young's biography available on http://www.jessecolinyoung.com/lip_release.htm. Websites accessed on April 18, 2005.

APPENDIX B: SUGGESTED COORDINATED LOCAL ACTIVITIES

1. The seven traditionally African American denominations are African Methodist Episcopal (AME), African Methodist Episcopal Zion (AMEZ), National Baptist Convention of America (NBCA), National Baptist USA-Inc. (NBC-USA), Progressive National Baptist Association (PNBA), Christian Methodist Episcopal (CME), and the Church of God in Christ (COGIC).

APPENDIX D: SUGGESTED COORDINATED DIASPORIC ACTIVITIES

1. There was a Maafa workshop at the St. Paul's Community Baptist Church, http://www. spcbc.com/, accessed on January 1, 2005. The article on Maafa is found at http://www.acfnewsource.org/religion/healing_ship.html.

additional resources
from Lora-Ellen McKinney

VIEW FROM THE PEW
What Preachers Can Learn from Church Members
Lora-Ellen McKinney
"One of the most insightful books on homiletics than perhaps has ever been written by a non-practitioner of the craft of preaching."
—Jeremiah A. Wright Jr., Pastor,
Trinity United Church of Christ,
Chicago, Illinois
Based on thorough research and numerous interviews of worshipers, this resource for a pastors and active laypersons provides a guide to preaching that is clear and effective and avoids unintended messages.
0-8170-1459-4 $13.00

TOTAL PRAISE!
An Orientation to Black Baptist Belief and Worship
Lora-Ellen McKinney, Foreword by H. Beecher Hicks
Provides information on Baptist beliefs, expressions of faith, and worship traditions in the African American context.
0-8170-1438-1 $14.00

CHRISTIAN EDUCATION IN THE AFRICAN AMERICAN CHURCH
A Guide for Teaching Truth
Lora-Ellen McKinney, Foreword by Johnny Ray Youngblood
Offers detailed practical guidance in virtually all areas of Christian education in the African American context.
0-8170-1450-0 $14.00

Also available from Judson Press:
CHURCH ADMINISTRATION IN THE BLACK PERSPECTIVE REVISED EDITION
Floyd Massey Jr. and Samuel B. McKinney
Covers all facets of administration for clergy and laity serving in black churches. Newly revised to include technology updates and financial planning information.
0-8170-1453-5 $15.00

Also available as a set:
THE MCKINNEY LIBRARY
Save 25% off the single-copy purchase price! Set includes Lora-Ellen McKinney's Total Praise! and Christian Education in the African American Church and Church Administration in the Black Perspective by Floyd Massey Jr., and Samuel Berry McKinney.
0-8170-1451-9 $33.00

www.judsonpress.com